Throw a Good Pass

Learning about Relationships with Help from Gramps and Dr. Stone

James Shaw

This book may be ordered by contacting James Shaw, PsyD, at www.drjshaw.com.

Because of the dynamic nature of the Internet, any Web addresses or links contained in this book may have changed since publication and may no longer be valid.

ISBN: 1500591009, ISBN-13: 978-1500591007

Printed in the United States of America

Disclaimer: The information, ideas and suggestions in this book are not intended as a substitute for professional advice. Before following any suggestions contained in this book, you should consult your personal physician or mental health professional. The author shall not be liable or responsible for any loss or damage allegedly arising as a consequence of your use or application of any information or suggestions in this book.

Author's note: This book is a work of fiction with the exception of historical facts and locations. Names, characters and incidents are the product of the author's imagination or are used fictitiously. Any resemblance to actual events or persons, living or dead, is coincidental.

*To my daughter, Janie,
who gives great effort to everything she
tries, finds value in relationships and is now
very successful.*

Contents

—✦—

Important Information about Narrators before Reading

I hope you really enjoy this book as the third and final book in the Help from Gramps series. To provide insight into three other characters' thoughts besides Tom Mochina, I decided to have three other characters narrate four chapters each in the first person. Due to this you might find that as the next chapter starts, it isn't perfectly chronological. For example, the first four chapters all start with Memorial Day weekend in 1972. I hope this doesn't bother you too much as you follow how these four different relationships progress to March 1973. Keep this in mind as you read.

Tom Mochina, who narrated *The Baseball Bat* and *Defensive End,* continues to narrate many of the chapters. Tom narrates all chapters that has a title doesn't contain the words, *Lucy*, *Luce*, *Roger*, or *Eve*. The chapters narrated by Lucy Davis have the words *Lucy* or *Luce* in their titles. The chapters narrated by Roger Franciszek have *Roger* in their titles. And the chapters narrated by Eve Mochina have the word *Eve* in their titles.

Thank you.

James Shaw

"School's out for forever,
School's out for summer,
School's out with fever,
School's out completely."
— *Alice Cooper (1972)*

Job Sharing

I t was Saturday, May 27, 1972.
I sprang out of bed, excited for my first day of work renting boats for Gramps' new business. I went out to the kitchen and poured some Count Chocula into a bowl, along with some milk. As I ate, I thought about how much fun this summer would be since I'd have a job to save for my dream car: the Mercury Capri.

Last summer Gramps had bought another lakefront property just down the lake from his house. Gramps is my neighbor who isn't related to me, but he likes me to call him Gramps. I've known him since I was nine years old, and he not only jokes around with me, he has given me sound advice on controlling my anger and anxiety and on how to communicate in more productive ways. I helped him, his son, Charlie, and his son-in-law, Jack, clear the land, build a boathouse, and erect some docks. Gramps had paid me a dollar an hour for my work.

I enjoyed being around Charlie as we worked. He's very knowledgeable in sports. He always has an opinion and the knowledge to back it up.

Trying to take a piece of property and turn it into a business is not very easy. Gramps, Jack and Charlie did not always agree on what to do.

1

Sometimes I thought they were mad at each other, but then one of them would start laughing. Charlie would make comments like, "Dad, you're getting so old, you can't think anymore." And Gramps would come back with, "Son, you were wearing diapers when I built my first dock."

Although most of the banter was between Gramps and Charlie, Jack and I got into it as well. Jack was teased for either moving too slow or coming up with some idea that Charlie and Gramps found ridiculous. Gramps told Jack that if he needed a consultant, he would have hired a gorgeous woman because the ideas would be about the same, but at least she'd be worth looking at. I tried my best not to be the butt of the jokes, but when I made a mistake, I would get something like, 'Tom, you're so good on the football field, but maybe construction just isn't your bag."

Sometimes Gramps would comment, "When I die, you will each have a third of this business, so pretend like it's yours now, and let's make it special. Tom, you'll have to marry Lucy to get your third."

Lucy was Gramps' youngest daughter, but she was still 14 years older than me, so that wasn't going to happen. But she was good looking. I never found it funny when Gramps joked about dying. I really wanted him to live forever.

Every day I left laughing, and we made great progress last summer. By the end of it, an empty lot was ready to be a business.

The property was now complete. It had three docks, a parking lot, a boathouse, several picnic tables, a boat ramp and a small, sandy beach area. Gramps' plan was to sell dock space to people with motorboats in the city and also to rent out rowboats and canoes.

I told my mother I was heading to work. The sign out by the road read, *Gramps' Boat Livery and Docking*, but mostly we just referred to it as *Gramps' Docks*.

I didn't want to cut through anyone's yard, so I walked along the road until I got to the sign and then walked down the road Gramps had built to get to the boathouse. When I arrived, he was already there.

"Tommy Boy, ready for some hard work?"

"I'm always ready."

"Good! Your job is to rent a boat to anyone who comes here. I'll work with you today so you get the hang of it. Then tomorrow, you're on your own. I'm going to pay you a dollar and thirty-five cents an hour. You'll work six hours per day after school is out. You want to work seven days a week, right?"

"Yes, I want to work as much as I can so I can buy a car when I'm sixteen."

"Great. Try to let me know in advance if you need to miss a day. So, once you're out of school, you'll work a nine am to three pm shift one day followed by a three pm to nine pm shift the next and alternate from there."

"That'll be great! Forty-two hours a week!" I said as I did the math in my head. "Will Stan be able to work the opposite shift?" I was always looking out for my best friend, who lived close by, right along the lake.

"I have someone for the opposite shift, but if Stan gets trained, he can fill in if either of you is out. My grandson, Todd, wants some hours too."

"What guy did you get for the opposite shift?"

"No guy! I talked to Hank and hired his granddaughter who will be staying with him this summer. She'll also work seven days a week. We'll have to train her."

"Teresa?"

"Yes, Teresa. Good, you know her! She's a hard-working young lady."

Gramps didn't let on that he knew I'd once considered Teresa my dream girl. Did he forget? He probably knew but wasn't saying anything. This was really a surprise. I wasn't sure what she thought of me now. I hoped this wouldn't be really uncomfortable.

"So, Teresa's going to be working the opposite shift of me?"

"Yes, she's fourteen, too, and probably saving for a car as well."

Two men who had just parked now walked toward us carrying fishing poles and tackle boxes.

"Hey, we saw the sign and were wondering if we could rent a boat," said one of the men.

"You've come to the right place. What are you fishing for today?" asked Gramps.

"We're hoping to catch some blue gill and maybe some largemouth bass."

"It's a dollar-fifty an hour or seven dollars for the whole day, plus fifty cents for each life preserver," said Gramps.

"We'll take one for the entire day."

"Come on in, and let's get you signed in. Just make sure you leave a few fish in the lake for the other people," Gramps joked.

He showed me how to sign them in and hold on to their driver's licenses until they brought the boat back. We put their names, the date and the current time in a notebook log.

"Tom, grab a couple cushions." Cushions served the dual purpose of being life preservers and something soft to sit on.

We then walked out on the dock where Gramps had twelve rowboats and two canoes.

Gramps led them to a boat out at the end of the dock, and I put the cushions on the seats. "Have a good time," he told them. "We need the boat back by dark!"

Once the men were paddling away, Gramps turned to me. "That's how you do it. The next one is yours."

After a few minutes, two other guys parked and walked toward us.

"Good morning! Welcome to Gramps'! Would ya like to rent a boat?" I asked, hoping to show Gramps how well I could do this.

"No, I have a speed boat and wanted to know what it would cost to dock it for the summer. The last few years I've taken it to Orchard Lake, but I had to trailer it and launch it each day I wanted to use it."

"Let me get Gramps."

Gramps talked to the men for about 5 minutes and then came walking back to me as the two men left.

"Did you lease them some dock space?"

"Nope! Those aren't the kind of people we want here. After I talked to them for a few minutes, they didn't seem honest. They might've been drug dealers."

"You still have some dock spaces open, right?"

"Not for them. I want this place to be for good, hardworking families. I don't have to lease dock space to just anyone. It has to be someone I think would fit in with the rest of the boat owners here."

A few minutes later, a man with two children walked up. "Welcome to Gramps'! Would you like to rent a boat or canoe?" I asked.

"Hello. Yes, I was thinking about renting a boat to row around the lake. Do you have children's life preservers available?"

"Yes, we have all sizes. The cost is a dollar-fifty an hour plus fifty cents for each life preserver."

"Great. I'll take a row boat for two hours."

"Please come on in the boat house and sign in. That'll be four dollars and fifty cents. How much does each child weigh?"

After a few minutes I got him all signed in and gave each child the appropriate life jacket and a cushion for the man. I showed them to their boat, and they were off.

"Great job, Tom! I knew I could count on you," Gramps said. "Do you think you could train Teresa when she gets here?"

"Of course."

"So what do you tell people who walk up and ask if there is dock space available?"

"Well, based on the people who were just here, I would say I don't handle that and they'd need to speak to Gramps."

"You got it, Tom. The best time to catch me is on the weekend between eight am and ten am. I'll try to be here during those times. I'll also be here from seven-thirty pm to nine pm on most days to help wash the boats. I'm excited about the grand opening tomorrow. Lucy is coming in from Chicago with her boyfriend. And don't worry," he continued. "I don't think things are going so well with them, so you've still got a shot with her."

I just smiled, knowing he was joking.

At around ten minutes to three that afternoon, Teresa came walking up. She was now about 5' 8"—just a couple inches shorter than me—and still looked absolutely great. She wore short cut offs, a tank top, and flip flops.

"Hi, Tom. I hear we get to work together this summer."

"Hi, Teresa. This should be a great summer. I'm so happy to have a job. Gramps asked me to show you how to rent the boats and what to say when people come up and want to lease dock space."

Teresa laughed. "He told me to call him Gramps, too. He's a funny guy!"

I showed her around the boat house and gave her thorough instructions on what to do in different situations. I was still very attracted to her. She was a beautiful girl, and there was something about her smile that made me smile when I looked at her. She had the softest-looking skin and still had really long hair. She just seemed so nice too!

"Teresa, I have a baseball game at five-thirty, so I have to go now. Is there anything else you need?"

"No! Thanks for showing me everything. I'll see you tomorrow!"

I walked away mesmerized. This was going to be a great summer. How could I find out if she was interested me? I had to make sure I wasn't going to get rejected. I decided it might be best to just be friends and co-workers for a while.

I got home and dressed for my Pony League game. We'd had a ten-win and thirteen-loss season, and this was our final game.

When I arrived, I saw Stan. "Tom, we should be able to get this one today. Let's finish the season strong!"

"If The Man's ready, The Machine's ready," I said with a big smile.

I looked at Stan, but he didn't smile back. "Where's the smile today?" I asked. "Summer's starting. Soon there'll be lots of bikinis to be seen."

"My parents aren't talking to each other. I get a little worried."

"Oh, man. Sorry to hear it. But don't think about that now. Let's get this game today."

Most of my friends seemed worried about their parents splitting up. I've never had that worry. I've always had to worry about my mom dating some jerk. Luckily she hasn't dated anyone in a while.

The baseball season had been fun, but the pitching had gotten a lot better and faster. I was hitting .410 on the year with two homeruns. Stan had told me he was hitting .615 with four homeruns. I was getting hits, but not at Stan's pace. His dad was still our coach and continued to bat us two-three in the order.

After a couple hours of play, we were trailing by one run with two out in the bottom of the seventh and final inning. Stan had just worked a walk, so it was up to me. The first pitch was a fastball over plate, but I took it so Stan could steal second. I now had a chance to tie the game with a base hit. The second pitch was a curve ball. I swung with everything I had, but the ball actually hit the plate. I hadn't even come close to hitting it. I stepped out of the box with a two-strike count. I knew I was thinking too much about ending the game with a homerun when I should be thinking about a base hit.

"Come on, Tom. Little rap now!" said Coach.

I was determined to get the bat on the ball. The next pitch was a fast ball inside, but somehow I thought it was a curve, and it took me by surprise. I let it go by because it seemed inside.

"Strike three!" roared the umpire.

I stood at the plate and didn't move. I put my head down and shut my eyes. The catcher had already left his position to congratulate the pitcher. What should I do? Should I start ripping into the umpire? Finally, I decided to just walk back to our bench with my head up. I was disappointed, but this was baseball. You can't get a hit every time, and you can't win every game. No one said anything to me.

Of course I wasn't happy about making the last out of the season. But I quickly appraised the situation and realized it was disappointing, but it really wasn't awful. It happened, and it was time to move on. I congratulated my teammates on our season and headed home.

On Sunday, I decided to go to work about an hour before my shift to talk to Teresa before she left.

"Hi, Tom. You're early."

"How do ya like the job so far?"

"It's easy, but there's no one to talk to most of the time. Gramps was here for a while this morning. He sold two more dock slips so it's been a good day. I rented eight boats. There are six still out."

"I came early 'cause I thought you might want some company."

"Yes, I'm so glad you came. I think next weekend I might bring my guitar and practice while it's slow. Do you play?"

"I always wanted to play guitar, but we haven't really had the money for lessons. I've been in the choir at school, though, and I can read music."

"Well, if you want, I can teach you guitar this summer. I really want to hear you sing."

"That might be a little embarrassing."

"I bet you're really good."

How can a girl this nice be this good looking? Wow, and she plays guitar! Just then a couple came walking up, and I turned to greet them.

"Now, Tom, I'm still on duty. I'll get them," Teresa told me. "Hello, I'm Teresa. Would you like to rent a boat?"

"Do you have any canoes?"

"Yes, we have a canoe available. How long would you like it?"

"Um, maybe three hours."

"Great! It'll be four dollars and fifty cents for three hours, plus fifty cents each for the life preservers."

I watched as Teresa took care of the entire rental and got them off on the lake.

"Are you working tomorrow?" I asked.

"No, Gramps said he'll be here for the afternoon shift tomorrow, but starting next Saturday, I'll be here every day. I still have four days of school."

Throw a Good Pass

"Break up to make up, that's all we do.
First you love me, then you hate me
That's a game for fools."
— The Stylistics (1972)

Luce Cannon

"**Y**ou said you were going to be here at seven-thirty! It's eight-fifteen!" I announced as I opened the door of my Chicago apartment.

"Luce, I had to do a few things. I'm here now. It's not that easy getting up on Saturday morning," said Mark, my boyfriend of seven years. He slouched in front of me, wearing shorts and a baggy t-shirt.

"Why does this happen every time? I thought we had a plan. I've been ready to go for an hour."

"What's the difference? We'll be fine."

"I hope so. Do you understand that I really hate it when you're late?"

"Man, I really tried to do something nice for you by driving to your parents' houses for Memorial Day weekend with you, and this is the thanks I get?"

"How long have you known me? How many times have I said I like to be on time? You're surprised by my reaction?"

"Can we go now? This is an important weekend. I need to talk to your father."

My eyes widened. Was he going to ask my father for my hand in marriage? What would my dad say? Would he just be polite and say yes? Does any dad ever say no? *My* dad knows this relationship has been a struggle.

"Okay, let's go. Here are my bags."

We loaded my suitcases into Mark's old Ford and headed up to Michigan. We didn't talk much, so I turned on the radio.

My family's great. My brother and sister are so nice, but sometimes it gets to me, seeing how they're married with children and such perfect families. I want children too, and both of them already had children by the time they were my age. Why haven't I found the perfect mate like them?

"Hey, Lucy! Let's play cops and coons."

I looked at Mark, squinting.

"Did you see that police car? It's one to nothing cops. Now, if you spot a dead raccoon on the side of the road, the coons get a point."

"We just passed something dead on the road."

"That didn't count because it wasn't clearly identifiable. You have to see the tail or the mask to be sure it's a raccoon."

Oh, *well*. We even argue about whether a dead animal's a raccoon. Mark can be very charming at times. He's good looking, and he's smart. I'm just not sure we're a good match. We disagree on just about everything, so I'm usually just frustrated with him. He means well, but I'm a Type A personality, and he's very Type B. He just doesn't care about winning. All of my friends think he's so great. But why don't *I* ever think that?

"Did you see the tail? That one was clearly identifiable. One to one," declared Mark.

"Both the term *cops* and especially *coons* sound derogatory. Let's at least call the game patrol officers and raccoons if we have to play."

"You find a way to ruin every game," Mark countered. "I tried to find something fun to do. I'm getting sick of your attitude."

I thought about telling him to turn back, but I really wanted to spend some time with my family, so I just sat and stewed.

After the four-hour drive to southeast Michigan, we first stopped in to see my dad and his wife, Ruth. My dad greeted us at the door and gave me a hug. He shook hands with Mark and invited us in.

Ruth came out and said hi to us too. She was a nice lady and always very kind to me. I hadn't liked Dad's second wife at all. He was married to her while I was in high school. I still wished Dad and my mom, his first wife, had stayed married, but it didn't work out that way, and I've adjusted to life with divorced parents.

"Dr. Davis, I would like to talk to you privately, if you have time?" said Mark.

My eyebrows rose, and I gave my dad a look of despair.

"Sure, Mark. Let's go out on the deck. It's beautiful out there."

My dad and Mark went outside, and I just sat inside, wondering what my dad would say.

"What are your plans for today?" asked Ruth.

"We can only stay a short time because my mother's expecting us, but we'll be back tomorrow for the grand opening party."

"Lucy, thank you so much for coming to town. It means so much for your father to have you here."

After a few minutes, Mark and Dad came in and went to my dad's study. Mark waited outside while Dad went in. When he returned he handed Mark something, which he took and put in his pocket. I looked at both of their faces, trying to determine what might have taken place, but they sat down and changed the subject to the grand opening.

After a little while, I told Dad we had to leave, and we headed out.

As we got in the car, I asked Mark, "So, how'd the conversation go with my dad?"

"Good."

"Good? Tell me what was said."

"I asked your dad if I could marry you, and he asked how we'd been getting along."

My eyebrows rose once again. "What'd you tell him?"

"I told him that I love you, but we've had some struggles. He asked that we attend couples counseling and get a psychologist's recommendation before he gave his permission to marry. He gave me the card of a psychologist who does some teaching at Michigan State and has office hours in Chicago on Mondays."

"Did you agree to this?"

"Yes, I think it's a good idea. We're going to be married a long time, and if this would help us have less conflict, I'm all for it. You have to learn to be less angry."

"Me? Maybe *you* need to learn to be less angry and start being responsible. Or maybe we'll just find out we're incompatible," I added, but after hesitating briefly, I said, "Fine. I'll do this. Give me the card. I'll call."

Mark handed me the card after digging it out of his pocked. "Dr. Marjorie Stone," I read.

I'd just put the card in my purse when we arrived at my mother's house. She had never remarried after her divorce from my father. It was always great visiting with her.

"Mollie and her family are coming for dinner," she announced as we came inside.

"Oh, great. I can't wait to see her and the kids."

Mark and I talked to my mother for a while, and then she said, "Oh, you two are so cute together. I can't wait to start planning another wedding."

"Mom!" My voice came out louder than I'd thought it would. "We're not ready yet. There's no rush!"

I didn't want to tell her about Mark's conversation with my dad or the counseling, and I hoped Mark wouldn't either.

"I'm sorry. It's just that you two look like you belong together."

I quickly changed the subject. "So, Mom, who's your latest boyfriend?"

"Lucy! There's no current boyfriend. I don't meet many men close to my age."

"Oh, come on, Mom! You work at William Beaumont Hospital, and the place must be crawling with attractive doctors."

"They're all married. And even if one was single, it would be unprofessional of me to approach a doctor in that way."

Just then there was a knock at the door, and my sister and her family arrived. I had fun catching up with her and her kids, while Mark mainly just talked sports with Jack, her husband. My mother made a great home-cooked dinner, and with all the people there, Mark and I didn't have to talk much with each other so there were no incidents.

The next day, after my mom made us lunch, we drove over to my dad's new lakefront property for the grand opening of Gramps' Docks. It was fun talking with all the people who rented dock space from dad, and Mark and I took out a canoe and paddled around.

When we got back, my brother Charlie and his family were there. He was talking to his friend Bernie.

"Hey, Bernie. How you doing? Get married yet?" I asked.

"Hi, Lucy. No, I keep busy at Ford but now that I have a place to dock my boat, I'm hoping to meet some ladies."

"Hey, good luck. Do I qualify as a lady? I want to go out on the boat." I turned and looked at Mark. "With Mark, of course."

Even though Bernie was four years older than me, I'd always had a crush on him. But I considered my brother's friends off limits.

A week later on Monday, Mark and I had our first appointment with the psychologist at her Chicago office. We signed in and waited in a small room until Dr. Stone came out and asked us to go back to her office. She was well dressed and looked good for a middle-aged lady. After introductions, she asked us if we had any questions, and I looked at Mark and replied that we didn't.

"Before we get into your current situation, I'd like to find out some background information for each of you. Would one of you start and tell me where you grew up, what your family life was like, how you did in school, higher education, jobs, a little about your friendships, and what kind of activities you were involved in."

I looked at Mark and quickly said, "I'll go first. I grew up in the West Bloomfield Township and went to Walled Lake schools. My parents divorced when I was just about to start kindergarten. I did really well in school and won awards for being a top student. I have an older sister and brother whom I'm very close to. I was the editor of the school newspaper, and I had a group of five friends who I hung out with throughout high school. I went on to the University of Michigan and got a degree in journalism. After college, I got a job with the *Chicago Sun-Times* where I'm a feature writer. I love my job, but someday I want to go back to Michigan, maybe work for the Free Press and write nonfiction books."

"Oh, that's great, Lucy. Thank you. Mark?"

"I grew up in Joliet. My parents are still together, and I'm the youngest of four boys. I played basketball and football in high school, and I went on to the University of Michigan and got a degree in business and a minor in engineering. My senior year, I met Lucy. I got a job at Illinois Central Railroad in management, and I'm now a shift operations manager."

"So, the two of you met at U of M? Tell me how you met."

I looked at Mark and then started speaking. "We were at a party, and Mark kept coming up to me and trying to get my number. I could tell he'd been drinking."

"What? That isn't what happened. You'd been drinking and kept staring at me."

"I didn't stare at you."

"You sure did, so I walked over and introduced myself."

"You came over to get my number, but I didn't give it to you. So you asked me to lunch on Monday, and we met at Student Union."

"As I recall, you asked me to the Union," Mark said.

"Let me stop you," Dr. Stone interrupted. "It sounds like you have different memories of how you met. Tell me this, Lucy, what do you like about Mark?"

I wasn't expecting that question. I came in ready to tell what I *didn't* like about him. "He's good looking." Mark smiled. "He can be nice at times. I know he really likes me and never looks at other women."

"Anything else?"

"Um, hmmm, I just can't think right now."

"Okay, thank you, Lucy. Mark, what do you like about Lucy?"

"She's the girl of my dreams. Look at her. She's gorgeous. I show her pictures to everyone. She's very intelligent. She's ambitious. Um, and she loves Wolverine basketball."

"So, Lucy, why'd you call to make this appointment?"

"I believe you know my father."

"Yes, Ray Davis is a wonderful teacher and physician."

"Mark asked my dad for permission to marry me, and my dad asked us to call you."

"Do you want to marry Mark?"

"Some days I do, but…most days I'm so frustrated with him that I don't."

"Lucy, what are you hoping to get out of these sessions?"

"I believe if Mark would be more responsible, we could be happy."

"Mark, what do you want to get out of these sessions?"

"I want Lucy to lighten up and not be so angry all the time."

"Tell me about a time Lucy got angry."

"Which time? How 'bout on the way to this session? She was mad about what I wore, mad about me being late to pick her up, mad that I was changing lanes too quickly, and now she'll be mad I brought these things up with you."

"Mark, what do you want Lucy to say to you when she's unhappy about things like these?"

"I don't want her to say anything. I just want her to be nice to me."

"Lucy, did you say anything nice to Mark when he picked you up?"

"No."

"He asked that you say something nice to him. We call this the 'soft startup'. Maybe something like this: 'Mark, thank you for picking me up. It's good to see you. Did you have a good day? I would rather you had worn a shirt that matched your pants.' Mark, would that have been better?"

"Much better." He looked down at his pants and shirt, probably trying to see why they didn't match.

"Lucy, is this something you could do?"

"Yes, I could. I'll try."

"We start with the soft startup, and then we do what I call 'throw a good pass'. You both like basketball. When a guard sees another player wide open under the basket, what does he do?"

"He passes him the ball," I said.

"Why?"

"Why? So he can score."

"Ah, so the guard's thinking the best chance to score is to pass the ball, and if the team scores, it's as good as him scoring himself. What happens if the guard throws the ball behind him or at his feet?

"He might not score," said Mark.

"Yes. So, Lucy, I want you to try this. After you do a soft startup when communicating with Mark about difficult subjects, try to throw the best pass you can so he catches it and scores."

"Maybe Mark should use the soft startup and throw me some good passes."

"I will," he assured me. "I think it's a great idea."

"We started talking today, but would you be willing to come back for the next three weeks? I have this time open."

We looked at each other and then Mark said, "It works for me."

"Yes, the next three weeks," I said.

"Great. I have a couple papers I would like you to read. One is about positive interactions in relationships and the other is about anger management. I have copies for both of you."

I glanced at the papers. The one on positive interaction was written by Dr. Stone. The one on anger management was written by my father. "My father wrote this."

"It's one of my favorite anger management papers, so I use it with my clients. I hope that's okay?"

I smiled.

"It was very nice to meet both of you. I look forward to seeing you next week."

"Thanks, Dr. Stone," we told her.

Roger's Neighborhood

H i! I'm Roger. What? You don't know me? Why should you? I never made it to the big leagues. I played minor league baseball for ten years. I played mainly with the St. Louis Cardinals organization, but after I slept through the start of a day game on the road, I was traded to the Cleveland Indians organization.

What a life! Playing baseball every day and going out every evening...I had dreams of being in the same outfield as Stan Musial. Every time I got a hit, I thought I'd get a call asking me to come up to the Cardinals, but it never happened.

My problem was that I liked women as much as playing baseball. Baseball was my ticket to get good-looking ladies interested in me. I would tell them I'd be playing for the Cardinals soon, and making lots of money. Many women were intrigued by me, and I always had my buddies to serve as my wingmen. I had a lot of girlfriends back then.

Late in my career, when I was playing in Indianapolis, I got a call from this one lady.

"Roger, it's Louise," she said.

"Louise, how great to hear from you!" I struggled to remember who Louise was and what she looked like.

"I'm glad you're in town. Can we meet tonight for dinner?"

Even though I wasn't sure who she was, the talent in Indianapolis was usually pretty good. If I didn't like what I saw after I met her, I could find a way to duck out.

"Sure, right after the game I'll meet you at Moore's Beer Tavern."

Moore's Beer Tavern, known today as the Slippery Noodle, was close to the ballpark. They served good drinks and good food, and there are bullet holes in the wall where John Dillinger used to take shooting practice.

After the game, I spiffed up a little and headed to the restaurant. A thin, wavy-haired lady approached me. "Roger."

Upon seeing her, I recognized her. We'd met a few months back and had a good time. I was glad she'd called me. It made tonight's job of picking up a lady so easy.

"Louise, how've you been? I've been meaning to call, but I get so busy on the road. Did you go to the game tonight?"

"No. Not tonight. How'd you do?"

"We lost to the Charleston Senators. Coach decided to give me the night off. I guess he thought I'd been working too hard." The truth was I'd barely played this year, and I'd been in the minors so long I probably wouldn't be asked to come back for another year.

We'd just started eating dinner when Louise said, "Roger, I'm pregnant."

I just looked at her, not knowing whether to say congratulations or I'm sorry. So I said nothing.

"I've only been with one man this year, so I'm pretty sure you're the father."

I was shocked. This was not the way I'd thought the evening would work out. But I decided to see her every night I was in town. I stayed away from Moore's after that night because it felt like Dillinger was shooting at me. But I did take her to St. Elmo's Steakhouse one night and the Grayland Hotel another night for dinner and music.

We stayed in touch, and after the season ended, I decided I should marry her, and it should be soon, given her condition.

I had gotten to know her parents, and they knew she was pregnant. I asked her father for her hand in marriage and explained that I had a job up in Michigan where I worked in the off-seasons. It would be my permanent job now since my baseball career was over.

So Louise and I got married and moved to a house in West Bloomfield Township, Michigan. I started working, and we waited for our child to be born.

I know you still don't know me. People in the community don't call me Roger. They know me as either Coach, Louise's husband, or Stan's dad. I could have been famous. I thought I was as talented as Stan Musial, but he made it and made it big. I was only known by the few fans who followed minor league baseball.

I've been married to Louise for 14 years, and our son is now 14 years old. I named my son Stan after the Cardinal great, Musial. I've had a lot of fun coaching Stan in baseball and basketball. He's really become a good baseball player and has a shot at the major leagues someday.

I've tried to be a good husband, but it's difficult to change after so many years of girl-watching. I still look at women. One of the women I find very attractive is Stan's friend Tom's mother. On hot days, she usually wears shorts and sleeveless shirts, and I'd sneak glimpses as I coached. I really like Tom. He's a hardworking kid, as well as a great friend to Stan, but I made sure he was on every team I coached because of his hot mother.

After many games, I would get an earful from Louise about me checking out other women. Of course I would deny this and tell her I was doing my best to coach the boys and found her accusations inappropriate. I certainly didn't want to admit she was right.

Louise and I barely speak anymore except to coordinate Stan's activities. We rarely touch each other. We don't even argue much anymore. We just go our separate ways. I really miss being affectionate, but it would be strange now if we tried after so many years of living our life this way.

"We need to talk," Louise told me after the television show ended. Stan had already gone to bed.

I just looked at her and said, "Okay."

"Baseball season will be over soon, and the summer is starting. I've really missed having a man in my life. Either you want to be my man again and stop sniffing every pair of panties you see, or I want a divorce."

"What about Stan?" I asked.

"What about Stan? It sounds like you're thinking about the divorce option. Stan'll be fine living here with me in this house. You can visit him and take him to his games."

I didn't know what to say. I really wanted to be free again to date any lady I wanted. And although I'd really like to latch on to Tom's mom, at this point it would be too weird given that the boys are best friends. But it'd sure be nice to trade this forty-year-old lady in for two twenty-year-olds.

Where would I live? I've gotten comfortable here. I have the neighborhood beach to park my boat. It would cost a lot more to get a second place. And I enjoy the meals Louise makes me. She really is a good mother to Stan.

"So, let's talk about the other option," I said slowly.

"The other option is that we go to marriage counseling and figure out how to get our marriage back on track."

"Marriage counseling?" I said, turning up my nose.

"Yes. When I had my forty-year annual checkup with Dr. Davis, he asked me about life in general, and I told him I thought our marriage was suffering."

"What? You told Dr. Davis our dirty laundry? How could you?"

"Dr. Davis highly recommended a psychologist he works with at Michigan State who works out of his office here on Thursdays. Her name's Dr. Marjorie Stone. Dr. Davis said she makes his referrals top priority."

"I need to think about this."

"Well, don't wait too long because if you don't decide to give this a try by the end of baseball season, I'm filing for divorce."

"Fine. Let's see her."

—✦—

The psychologist was able to get us in the following Thursday. I wasn't excited about the appointment, but I wasn't excited about losing my son either.

"Good afternoon. You must be Louise Franciszek," she said as she shook Louise's hand. Then she turned to me. "Hi, I'm Dr. Marjorie Stone."

"Hi, I'm Roger." She was good looking for an old lady.

"Come right this way to my office."

We followed her.

"Before we get started, do either of you have any questions for me?"

"Yes. So why do you practice in this area and Chicago while teaching in East Lansing?" I said, hoping to delay her asking us questions.

"Good question. It's unusual. I first got the job at Michigan State, and I wanted to practice, so Dr. Davis invited me to practice here. Then I got married, and my husband's from the Chicago area, so I started a practice there near my home. But I kept my job at MSU and still love my practice here one day a week. Any other questions?"

"How can you stand hearing about other people's problems every day?" I asked.

"I love this job. I feel a great reward in helping people find solutions. Now my turn. Before we get into your current situation, I'd like to find out some background on each of you. Would one of you start and tell me where you grew up, what your family life was like, how you did in school, higher education, jobs, a little about your friendships, and what kind of activities you were involved in."

"I'll go first," said Louise. "I grew up in Noblesville, Indiana. I have an older sister and a younger brother. I never went to college. I worked as a waitress in Indiana until I got married to Roger. He had a job up here in Michigan, so I moved up here and didn't have to work. I just raised our son Stan. I like to cook and sew."

"Thanks, Louise. Roger?"

"I grew up in Hamtramck. My parents had immigrated from Poland. I have two younger sisters, and I played high school basketball, football and baseball and got offered a professional contract to play in the St. Louis Cardinal organization out of high school, so I played baseball until I was twenty-eight. I work for Pontiac Motors, and I hate my job, but I enjoy coaching my son in sports. He's very talented and has a good chance to be a major league shortstop."

"So how'd the two of you meet?"

We both hesitated, and then Louise spoke up. "We met at a bar. Roger was so charming. We ended up going back to his place to...to get to know each other better. I guess we got to know each other too well because I became pregnant with Stan."

"You got pregnant on the night you met?" said Dr. Stone raising her eyebrows. "So Louise, you called me for the appointment. How can I help you?"

"We have no relationship. I cook for him. I wash his clothes. But we don't talk. We don't touch. We both just raise our son. I want a relationship again."

"Do you want a relationship with Roger?"

"I'm not sure. I don't know if it's possible. I don't think that I'm what Roger wants. I see him looking at other women, but he doesn't look at me."

"Now, Weezy, that's not true."

"You haven't called me that in five years. Why now? Oh, we're in therapy, right? You have to impress the psychologist."

"What? You don't listen."

"Let me stop you, because arguments are not productive," said Dr. Stone. "Roger, what do you want out of this?"

"I want to keep my son...I mean my family."

"You had it right the first time," snapped Louise. "You want your son. You don't want me. But you can't just have your son. We're a package deal."

"I just don't understand why Louise would say we don't have a relationship. I work hard. I do a lot around the house. I'm kind to her."

"Oh, please! If we're going to get anything out of this, you have to be honest. You're not kind to me! You don't even touch me. You probably have several other girlfriends."

"Dr. Stone, do you see what I'm up against? She's delusional."

"So, Roger, let me clarify. You want to stay with Louise, and you're willing to work toward a better marriage?"

"Hmmm, I'm not sure. I gave her the best years of my life, and this is how she acts. I think I want out."

"Well, I want out too! Dr. Stone, I don't know this man. He's putting on an act for you."

"I can only help the two of you if you want my help. Let me ask both of you again if you want to try to stay together and are willing to try some ideas I have."

We both agreed to try.

"Roger, when you go to work, do you hug and kiss Louise and tell her you care for her?"

"Dr. Stone, he never tells me he loves me and doesn't touch me at all."

"Roger?"

"When I leave for work, Louise is sleeping so I don't want to bother her."

"Let's try this. Would it be okay if you touch her on the back and give her a kiss on the cheek before you leave?"

"Sure, I'll do it if I don't get yelled at."

"I won't yell at you if you do that. I'd like it."

"Great. Would you do this every day?"

We both agreed.

"Now, what kind of greeting do you give each other when you get home from work?"

No one said anything.

"Would you be willing to give a five-second hug and a brief kiss when you get home?"

"I'm not sure how we'd do that. I don't know where she is when I get home," I said.

"I'm usually in the kitchen."

"How would I know that?"

"Here's what I want you to do. Louise, if you hear Roger getting home, go to the front door.

Roger, if Louise isn't at the front door, go find her and give her the hug and kiss."

"All right, I can do it," I said. "Are we just about done?"

"Not quite. Earlier I thought Louise told me that you don't communicate. I want you to spend five minutes each night talking to Louise with her truly listening and understanding what you are saying. Then I want her to talk for five minutes and, Roger, I want you to listen and understand what she is saying. Also, Roger, I want you to ask Louise on a date, and if she accepts, please take her. Lastly, I have a short paper on positive interaction in relationships that I wrote and would like each of you to read."

She looked back and forth between us for a moment. "What did you think of your first couple's session? Are you willing to try this?"

"I will," said Louise with a smile. "And I'd love to go on a date."

"And it's whispered that soon if we all call the tune,
Then the piper will lead us to reason.
And a new day will dawn for those who stand long,
And the forests will echo with laughter."
— *Led Zeppelin (1971)*

Memorial Day Eve

I was born Helenka Éva Mochina on August 4, 1939, in Hungary. My parents had been through many wars after Austria split from Austria-Hungary and the Czechs, Romanians and Serbs gained control of parts of Hungary. With the start of World War II, in 1942, my father and many other Hungarian men decided to move their families to Michigan, just two years before the invasion and bombing of Budapest.

My parents told me my American name would be Helen, because if I kept my given name, I would be discriminated against. I went by Helen for many years, but lately I've decided to go by Eve. I don't remember a lot of those early days in Michigan, but I somehow was able to learn both languages. My parents insisted on English being spoken in our home, but when we had gatherings of friends and family, we spoke Hungarian.

In high school, I started dating the most handsome Hungarian man, Albert. I dreamed that we would be together always. The summer after high school, I found out I was pregnant. I was excited that Albert and I would have a family of our own.

Although I had only been with one man,
Albert accused me of cheating on him and told me
he didn't want anything else to do with me. When I
told him I had only been with him, he said I was
lying. He started dating other women, and I was
heartbroken.

I raised my baby, Thomas, with the help of
my parents for about five years, and I didn't date
much during that time. I guess having a child
made me unattractive to men. In 1963, I moved
out to a small house in the suburbs to raise my
child without my parents and to get Thomas away
from the city. I found a church home but didn't
find the man of my dreams like I'd hoped.

However, my son established some good
friendships and good role models. He's done well
academically and in sports. I don't think he even
minds living in this shack. I guess he's gotten used
to it. I haven't.

I hate this house and everything about it. It
doesn't have a shower or garage, and the floor
creeks when we walk. I don't even have a washer
and dryer like most others. There must be a better
life. What do all these other women who live in
their middle-class homes have over me?

Do I need a degree to get a husband? None
of these other women have one. I couldn't believe
Louise got pregnant at the same time as me but
Roger stepped up and married her. Albert refused
to raise his son. He still calls me every once in a
while, hoping to go out with me, but I don't go,
and I don't tell Tom. I've asked him so many times
to come to one of Tom's games, but he's never
shown up. Why can't he be in involved in his son's
life like Roger? Why can't I have a relationship like
Louise and Roger do?

I know I'd have more in common with a Hungarian man, but there aren't any I like. Maybe I should talk to Dr. Davis and see if he could set me up with one of his doctor friends. I can't believe Dr. Davis' son is my age. I wish I'd met him before he got married. He's a real man, and Tom likes him.

Tom still has four years of high school. Should I wait until he graduates to find a man? He doesn't seem to like most of the men I meet. Working as a trucking dispatcher, I meet truckers. I wish I had some skills to get a better job.

I've taken a night class the last two semesters at Oakland Community College. Maybe I could get a better job. And I don't understand why I haven't met any men at the church. They're all married.

On Saturday, I walked down to the lake and sat on a picnic table. I knew Tom would be over at the new property. Dr. Davis saw me and walked over.

"I'm so used to seeing a boy sitting here, and now I have a beautiful lady on the picnic table."

"Dr. Davis," I said, blushing. "I actually came down here to seek your advice."

"I'm sorry. If you call me Dr. Davis, I have to check your heart and lungs. If you want advice, you have to call me Gramps," he said with a smile.

"Okay, Gramps," I said, trying to control my laughter. "I'm lonely for a man."

"Helen! I'm flattered, but I'm taken. Ruth is a wonderful wife."

I laughed and laughed. He's so funny.

"I'm thirty-two! No offense, because you're a handsome man, but I would like to find a man under forty. Oh, and, Dr. Davis, I go by my middle name now, Eve. Everyone seemed to want to shorten my first name to one syllable and with Helen, well, you know..."

"Yes, I can see why you wouldn't want the shortened form of your name. I'll call you Eve, but you have to start calling me Gramps, okay?"

"Okay."

"It's difficult at your age. I don't know any single men at the church. Hmmm...I could ask Mollie or Charlie. Wait a minute—one of Charlie's friends leased a boat slip from me. He has two children who are probably in early elementary school. He likes to take them out on the boat."

"If he has young children, where is his wife?"

"She died."

"How?"

"She developed a severe pneumonia, and they couldn't save her. It was very tragic. She's been gone about three years."

"Were you her doctor?"

"No, I believe her doctors were in Detroit. I know she died at Henry Ford Hospital."

"I feel really bad for him."

"He has a good job at Ford Motor. He's coming to the grand opening party tomorrow. Are you planning on coming?"

"I hadn't planned on it. It's embarrassing to come alone."

"He—, I mean Eve, this will be an opportunity to meet people. I hope you'll come. If you'd like, I'll talk to him and let him know you're coming."

"Okay, Doc—" I smiled. "Gramps, I'll be there. What's his name?"

"Guy," Gramps said with a smile.

"Guy?"

"Yes, the guy's name is Guy." We both laughed.

The next day I walked to the new docks where they were having the grand opening, even though I hated going there by myself. Tom was working there, so I decided that my excuse for going was to see my son's new job. When I arrived, I saw a group of people, but I kept walking over near Tom.

"Hey, Mom, want to take a boat out? It's fun."

"I wouldn't know how to row it. Maybe you could take me."

"Hey, I'm on the job right now, but some other time. Why'd you come down?"

"I just wanted to see where you worked. I thought this might be a good time since Gramps invited me for the grand opening."

"Gramps?" Tom laughed.

"Yes, I know he must like to be called Gramps since he named this place Gramps."

Tom looked at me suspiciously but then went on to explain what he did on the job.

"Gramps told me I could get dinner here," I told him after a few minutes. "So I'm going over to look at the food."

I walked straight to a friendly face.

"I'm so glad you could make it. Gramps tells me you go by Eve now," said Ruth.

"Yes, thanks for inviting me."

"We have plenty of food, so please make yourself a plate."

I got a hotdog and some chips, but I was too embarrassed to eat the corn-on-the-cob in front of people. I sat down at a table far away from anyone else. As I was eating, a lady I didn't know approached me.

"Hi, do you have a boat here?"

"No, my son works here, so I just came to see it."

"Well, nice meeting you," she said as she left.

I guess I'm nobody if I don't own a boat here. How embarrassing. I decided to finish up my food and leave.

Just as I finished eating and stood up, Charlie walked over. "Hi, Helen. Don't leave so soon."

"Hello! I know this is confusing, but I now go by Eve. Helen is too formal. And I have a lot to do today."

"I want ya to meet one of my good friends. He has a boat here. In fact, he's out sitting in his boat. Would you like to come out?"

I was struck with terror. *Was this Guy?*

"I'd probably be too nervous. I better go."

"Five minutes. Please."

"You're twisting my arm. Okay."

We walked out on the dock and approached the boat.

"Eve, meet Bernie."

I stuck out my hand to shake his. He held it for several seconds.

"Have we met before?"

"No, I don't think so." I was shaking a little. He had such a young-looking face. His smile was captivating, and I couldn't look away from his eyes. He was tall and looked athletic. There was something about his legs that seemed so shapely.

"My real name is Guy Burns, but Charlie and the guys call me Bernie. You have a very athletic and intelligent son. Charlie told me about some of his football games, so I went to see him play a couple years ago. Yes! That's where I saw you."

I just kept staring at how good looking he was. *This is Guy! Wow!* Why would he want to talk to me? "Well, baseball season just ended, and he doesn't have football games until September. He'll be playing for the high school this next year."

"I'm going to plan on trying to make the first game."

I smiled, not sure what to say. "Well, I'd better go. Nice meeting you, Guy."

"It was a pleasure."

I hustled down the dock and walked home. Why hadn't I stayed and talked to him more? I didn't really have anything to do. Tomorrow was Memorial Day, and I had the day off work. I had my chance to meet him, and I blew it. He probably thinks I don't like him.

I went back home, called one of my Hungarian friends and told her about Guy. She told me she was sure he was going to call me. But how could he? He doesn't have my number. She was so excited.

Later that evening Tom was still down at the boat house, and I was watching TV when the phone rang. It figured must be my mother wondering if we were coming to the city to see her. But I'd already told her Tom was now working. I picked up the phone. "Hello?"

"Eve? This is Guy."

"Guy, how are you? Are you still at the lake?"

"No, I'm back in Dearborn, but I'm coming out tomorrow. I was wondering if you'd want to come on the boat with me. I'm packing a cooler for lunch."

"Yes, that sounds fun. What time would you like me to meet you?"

"Would eleven-thirty in the morning work? Wear your bathing suit in case you want to jump in.

"Sure. See you then."

I hung up and felt very nervous about telling Tom I was going on the boat with Guy. How would he react? I decided I had to tell him because he would see me there.

But to my surprise, when he came home and I told him, he barely reacted. He just seemed focused on himself and being there for his job. He must have had something on his mind. When I asked him what was new, he told me about Teresa working at Gramps' too and how he could see her every day. I couldn't bring myself to tell him my reaction to meeting Guy had been so similar to when he first met Teresa.

The next day, Memorial Day, I walked over to the dock where Guy kept his boat. I had my bathing suit on, but I wore shorts and a shirt over it.

"Hi," I said as I approached the boat.

"Eve, so glad you made it. You look great!" Guy said, and he just kept looking at me. "Have you been around the lake?"

"No, I've lived here nine years and have not been out on the lake."

"Well, let's take a ride around the lake before I pull you skiing."

"What? Skiing?"

Guy just laughed.

As we traveled down to the west end of the lake, I said, "So, Charlie's dad told me you have two children, and you lost your wife." I could tell I'd surprised him with my comment.

"Yes, my wife died three years ago. It was very painful. There was a long grieving process, and I was angry and depressed. It wasn't supposed to be that way. We were supposed to be together until old age. I didn't think I could ever date again, and I just wanted to raise my son, Carl, who's now six, and my daughter, Karen, who will turn four later this summer. It took a long time, but now I realize that she's gone, and it's okay if I meet someone new."

"I couldn't even imagine going through something like that." I looked at him and could tell it was tough for him to tell me. "Where are your children today?"

"They spend some holiday weekends with their mother's family, so they're in Dearborn today. They have cousins there who they play with." He paused for a moment and then looked at me again. "So, you found out about me. Now tell me why a gorgeous lady like you is still single. I'm stunned that a thousand guys haven't tried to swoop you up."

"I've had a lot of men ask me out, but I haven't found that really comfortable situation yet. It has to work for me and for...my son, Tom."

We took the boat under a road, and Guy told me we were no longer on Upper Straits Lake but were now on Middle Straits Lake. We traveled around this lake and saw a place where they were building houses.

"This is the West Acres neighborhood," he said. "I'd love to buy a house on this lake, but it would be a long drive to work."

I nodded and relaxed back into the boat. I was having such a great time. For a moment, I dreamed about living in one of these nice lake homes with Guy.

"Summer breeze makes me feel fine,
Blowing through the jasmine in my mind."
— *Seals and Crofts (1972)*

My Girl

O n Tuesday, I had to finish up my last week of school, and I was distracted thinking about Teresa. I went to lunch and met up with my friends: Stan, Denny, and Floyd.

"How's that job going? Any hot chicks over there or are they all over at Stan's beach? Denny and I might have to take the long bike ride to check out the bikinis," said Floyd.

Stan seemed distracted and not wanting to talk.

"My girlfriend from four summers ago is now working the job with me," I told him. "She's hot but she's all mine."

"Hey, when we meet some girls, can we borrow one of those row boats to take them out on the lake?" asked Denny.

"I'll have to ask Gramps. My job is to collect the money for boat rental."

"Maybe we'll cruise up and down Stan's beach. What do think?" asked Floyd, turning to Stan.

"Sure," said Stan, but he still looked disturbed.

"Let's meet up next week. You up for the bike ride?" Floyd said looking at Stan and Denny.

On the bus ride home, I could tell Stan was still distracted, so I offered to get off at his house and have his mother take me home after we'd had a little time together. He agreed, and we walked to the beach.

"Hey, man, you moved way ahead of me in baseball this year," I told him. "We just have three days of school left. Everything okay?"

"My parents are divorcing. I overheard them talking about it. I knew they weren't getting along great, but I didn't think it would happen. I might have to move. And I was so excited about playing sports with you at Walled Lake Central."

"Wow, I can't imagine you moving out of the school district. They said you were moving?"

"Well, they didn't exactly say we were moving, but that's what happens when parents divorce. Remember what happened to Joe when his parents divorced?"

"We never heard from him again."

"Exactly."

"Stan, I've been daydreaming a lot about Teresa, but this doesn't even compare to what you're going through. I've got a proposal for you."

"What's that?"

"I will try not to think about Teresa until Friday if you try not to think about your parents' issues until Friday, and we'll both try to ace our eighth-grade finals this week. Then when we get out of school on Friday, we can think about this stuff as much as we want. How does that sound?"

"Oh, man, you're right. I've been sitting around when I should be studying."

"Maybe by Friday your parents will have it worked out."

"Let's do it. A week of studying and then a summer to have fun," said Stan.

—◆—

Stan and I kept to our plan and reminded each other several times throughout the week. We both ended up making the Dean's List. On Friday after school, I got off the bus at Stan's house. We grabbed his football and headed to his neighborhood beach.

"Well, my parents are still together," he told me. "Everything's been quiet this week. Maybe they were just angry! Come on, throw me the ball."

We played catch for a while and then a group of older girls walked up to the beach. I had to look carefully because they were dressed in shorts and shirts, not bikinis, but I couldn't miss Rocky's hair. As I made eye contact with her, Stan threw me the football, and I had to duck or it would have beaned me in the head.

Rocky started laughing. "Hey, girls, here are the two jocks of the beach. Tom, you're so tall now."

We talked to them for a few minutes and then they kept walking, and we kept throwing the football. After a while we stopped.

"Tom, Rocky's looking fine. I bet you want to see her this summer."

"Rocky's a beautiful lady, but I only want one girl this summer: Teresa."

Stan's eyes got big. "You mean to tell me if Rocky wanted to be your girlfriend, you wouldn't want her?"

"Remember the school dance a few years ago? We had to decide who we wanted because if we chose wrong, we would lose out on the girl we really wanted. I'm not going to lose out on Teresa chasing every fine lady I see."

"Man, you must really be into her. Denny and Floyd will think you're crazy!"

— ✦ —

The next day, Teresa had the morning shift, but I ventured down around 12:30. I found her playing her guitar.

"Hey, Tom," she said in her quiet voice.

"Teresa, keep playing, you sound great."

She played the introduction to "Stairway to Heaven." When she got to the point where the lyrics would start, I started singing.

"There's a lady who's sure all that glitters is gold, and she's buying a stairway to Heaven. When she gets there she knows if the stores all are closed, in a word she can get what she came for."

"Tom, you're so good. You sound just like Led Zeppelin."

"I sing this song a lot. I have a knack for singing songs so much that I remember the words. How'd you learn how to play that?"

"It takes a lot of practice. Do you want to try?"

She handed me the guitar, but a couple guys who'd been out fishing had just come in, so she went out to tie up the boat.

As the guys came in, they looked at me holding the guitar and asked if I knew any Eddie Arnold. My mother had one of his albums, so I actually did know the songs. I took one strum of guitar and sang, "What's he doing in my world? Did you tell him that you're my girl? If he's not more than just a friend, then why were you kissing him?"

The guys started applauding. I knew nothing about the guitar but successfully faked it by singing.

As the guys left, Teresa said, "Oh my! You can sing, but that was no chord. You need to at least learn a few chords if you're going to fake it."

She showed me E minor chord, which seemed simple enough. This was the chord Neil Young uses to start "Heart of Gold." At least it was music. We had fun, but at first it was hard for me just to press the strings down.

She taught me how to play "Happy Birthday" because she thought it would be a good place to start, so I played it over and over. I learned one octave, which was enough to play basic songs.

We had a fun week, and I spent much of my off time with her. When I worked and she wasn't there, I worked on my horseshoe game and, of course, sang along with the radio. I also worked on my tan.

Late Wednesday afternoon, Stan, Denny and Floyd came to visit on their bikes. They wanted to take some boats out, but Gramps had told me he wanted to meet them first because he'd only met Stan. Gramps and the guys hit it off, but he laid down the rules about respecting the boats and said he didn't want any horseplay.

To my surprise, the guys were very good with the boats. They just wanted to race each other to find out who was the fastest. Denny was the fastest of the three, but he would still need to race me sometime before fully claiming his championship.

We had a lot of fun and also played horseshoes. I could play horseshoes while working, but I couldn't go out in the boats and miss customers. We played three games each with a different partner, but I won all three games. They tried to call it my home field advantage, but the bottom line was that I'd practiced every day and gotten good at it.

On Saturday, I finished up work at 3:00 but Teresa came on, so I stayed and talked to her. At about 3:20, a group of older guys came up to rent a boat. They started complimenting Teresa on how good she looked, and she clearly enjoyed the attention. However, I didn't like it. She looked really happy—even happier than she was with me, and I started to realize where I stood with her.

She collected the money, and while she was showing the guys to their boat, I left for home without saying goodbye. I didn't go back there until about ten minutes before my shift started the next day.

"Tom, where'd you go?" she asked me. "You left while I was renting a boat!"

"You were busy, and I was ready to go home."

She looked at me sadly. "I thought we were friends. I was very hurt that you didn't say goodbye."

"You didn't look hurt. In fact, you looked pretty happy."

"I was renting a boat. We're supposed to look happy renting a boat."

I didn't know what to say to that, so I just said, "Well, I'm here to work."

"I don't know why you're acting like this. We've gotten along so well. I've never seen you like this. I'm leaving." She gathered up her stuff.

"Goodbye. I don't want you to leave without saying goodbye," I said.

She turned and looked at me. I couldn't tell if she was mad or sad, but she didn't look happy. I'd hurt her.

I looked at her and said, "I'm sorry. You're right. I'm being a jerk." I started to tear up a little but knew I had to continue. "It's been so much fun with you this summer, and I started to think of you as my girlfriend even though I know you're not. I got jealous seeing you with those guys. You're not my girlfriend. It was stupid. Do you forgive me?" I put my head down, thinking that would be a way not to control any unwanted tears.

"Tom, that's the sweetest thing anyone's ever said to me. Could we hug?"

I'd been waiting for the chance to hug her, but instead of enjoying having her in my arms, I had to wipe my eyes so she wouldn't see any tears.

She pulled away a little so we could look at each other and said, "Tom, I've wanted to be your girlfriend for four years. This week has been so special. I'm sorry I got carried away with those guys. I hope I didn't mess this up between you and me."

"You didn't mess it up, I did." I told her. "I know better. Gramps has worked with me on anger control. I knew this was a three on the scale. I knew you should laugh with those guys because they were customers. What I need to sort through is that you're good looking not just to me but to everyone. I'm going to have to get used to guys flirting with you."

"Thank you. I hope you know this works both ways. You're a great-looking guy. It's difficult for me to see the girls look at you. Tom, I want to be your girlfriend. I don't want to shop for any other guys."

"That's what I want to. Stan thought I was crazy the other day when Rocky was talking to me, and I told him I only wanted you."

We looked at each for a moment and had started to move closer together when we heard Gramps say, "How many boats did we rent today?"

"Hi, Gramps, I'll have to go look. Teresa rented all of the boats today."

"We rented eight boats and two canoes," said Teresa.

"Wow. How much do the two of you owe me for working here?"

I knew Gramps was joking around, but I did owe him something for helping me meet this really great girl.

"Hey, you owe *us*," said Teresa. "We rented a lot of boats."

Gramps smiled so I said, "You agreed to pay us fifty-six dollars and seventy cents for the week."

"Tom, you're so good at math. I'll tell you what, you two have really had a good week." He pulled out a roll of twenties and handed us each three bills. "You both worked last weekend too." He then handed us each another $20. "Is this enough?"

We thanked him and told him how much we enjoyed working here. Then Teresa left to go home.

"How's everything going?" Gramps asked when we were alone. "Do you enjoy working with Teresa?"

"She's very special and becoming a really good friend," I told him. "We had a little issue this week when I got jealous of her talking to guy customers. I think we worked through it, though."

"It looked like you were going to kiss her when I walked up."

"I really like her," I said, smiling.

"I could tell you like her. I remember you once called her your dream girl. I thought the two of you might hit it off."

He had remembered.

"Did Teresa tell you why she's staying out here this summer?" he asked me.

"I thought it was for this job."

"Her mother and stepfather broke up, so her grandfather Hank invited her and her mom to live with him for the summer until she settled the divorce and got her own house. When he told me this, I decided to give her this job to take her mind off of the situation."

"I had no idea. She didn't tell me anything about this."

"Maybe she will in time. Don't push her. I'm sure it's not easy to uproot from your home. At least they waited until school was out so she has time to adjust."

"Tom, if you and Teresa decide to do the girlfriend–boyfriend thing, you have to agree that you'll remain friends if you decide to break up. You will still have to work together. The basis for any romantic relationship is friendship. If you're not friends, you don't have a relationship."

"I'll talk to her about this. She is my friend, and I don't want to mess that up."

Gramps then smiled and changed the subject. "Who's the king to the classroom?"

"The teacher?"

"No, the ruler," he said with a smile. "And who's the ruler of this beach?" He pointed to the sandy area.

"I'm sure you are."

"No, it's you. You're the sun of the beach!" He shocked me on that one, like he always seemed to do. It made the rest of the day go well.

— ✦ —

That evening, Gramps had left, and I was relaxing on the picnic table. It was about 8:00 and all of the boats were in, but I was scheduled to stay until 9:00. Just then Teresa came walking up.

"Hey," I said.

"Hey. I got home and just felt there was some unfinished business," she said sternly.

"Teresa, I said I was sorry."

"I know. But we were talking about being girlfriend–boyfriend, and we got interrupted."

"I want you more than anything to be my girlfriend, but most of all, I want you to be my friend, and I don't want us to lose the friendship if being my girlfriend doesn't work out."

She looked at me, seeming a little confused at first, and then she said, "Yes, friends forever, but let's try the boyfriend thing."

"We're on the same page."

"Not quite. We still have unfinished business. What were you going to do when Gramps walked up this afternoon?"

I smiled and allowed her to come and embrace me, but then I said, "Wait!"

"What?"

"We agreed to be friends first and boyfriend and girlfriend second. Let's wait a month before we kiss."

"Tom, why? Can we hold hands?"

I grabbed her hand and held it. "I know this sounds strange, but if we're still feeling the same way in a month, I think we will really have something special."

Cut Luce

T he telephone rang.

"Hey, it's Luce." I knew Mark's pattern, so I assumed it was him.

"Lucy?"

"Oh, hi, Dad. How are you?"

"I live on this beautiful lake and have three wonderful adult children. Life couldn't be better. How are you?"

"Mark and I went to see Dr. Stone." There was a moment of silence. "She's a nice lady. I'm just not sure I got a lot out of it."

"It's only the first visit. It was probably just an information-gathering session."

"Guess what?"

"You got promoted again?"

"No, Dad. She gave me a copy of your paper on anger control and wants me to read it."

"I've told you the story about anger control many times."

"I know. But she must think I have an anger problem. Do you think I do?"

"Lucy, my paper says the nicest people tend to get angry because other people aren't as nice as them, and they expect everyone to be that nice."

"I don't think that's why she gave me the paper. Mark told her I got angry four times in one day! "

"Mark gave you, and her, some information. You don't have to agree with it, but you should try to understand what he's telling you. Only you know if you got angry. Did your heart rate increase?"

"No, I don't think so. I think he confuses suggestions as anger."

"Maybe when Mark reads the paper, you can explain that you don't get angry, you just criticize when he doesn't do what you want."

"Oh my. When you put it that way, it sounds really bad. I criticize my boyfriend because he doesn't do what I want. I *do* that. I know I do."

"Yet he wants to marry you. He's ready to commit his life to you."

"Have you heard of *soft startup* and *throw a good pass*?"

"Yes, *soft startup* is from Gottman's work and *throw a good pass* is from Dr. Stone."

"Should I try these?"

"Luce, that's up to you. Good luck with it. I'll call you next week to see if you got your promotion."

"Okay, Dad. Thanks for calling."

Just as I got off the phone with Dad, it rang again.

"Hey, it's Luce."

"Hey, you've been on the phone."

"Yes, Dad called."

"Did he ask about the session?"

"He wouldn't do that, but I wanted to see what he thought. I know Dr. Stone wanted me to read the anger paper, but it's important that you read it too. I know I'm not always nice. Let me know when you've read both papers."

"Okay. How was your day?"

"It was actually pretty good. I got the interview I've been trying to get for a week. How was yours?"

"No crashes. All is well. What days did you want to get together this week?"

"Well, I have a lot of work this week. Just let me know later in the week if you have any ideas."

"Okay. Goodnight."

"Goodnight."

I stopped and thought about the conversation. Why did I not agree to get together? I thought about it for a while, and then it hit me. Mark just wanted to come over and sit around and watch sports on my TV. He didn't offer to take me out or come up with any creative idea. He just doesn't make me feel special. I want to feel really special. This is what I need to bring up at the next session.

—✦—

When Monday came, we went to visit Dr. Stone again. After she greeted us, she asked if there was anything positive about the week.

"Yes," I said, "I got some great interviews and articles written, and I went for three runs outside."

"Mark?"

"I can't think of anything. I only got to see Luce on Sunday when I watched the White Sox game on TV."

"So you two only see each other once a week outside of session?"

"No, it's usually like four times," said Mark.

"Why only once this week?"

"That's the way Lucy wanted it."

"Mark didn't call with any plans to do anything, and I had better things to do than have him over and sit and watch sports on TV," I said.

"Did either of you read the material I gave you?"

We both nodded. "I read my Dad's anger paper," I said. "He first told me about anger control when I was nine." I smiled. "I think I live my life around not allowing myself to get angry. I use these techniques successfully."

"What? This paper had to be written about you," Mark interjected.

"Mark, would you please listen to me before you say that? I understand it's in your head that I get angry, and you can't get it out, but the paper doesn't describe me. I keep my heart rate under control with my thinking strategies. My fault's that I criticize without using the soft startup or throwing a good pass. I didn't think I had to. I thought as adults I could just tell it to you straight, but after reading the relationship paper, I realized there are many things I don't do well. This week I stonewalled you, so I didn't allow for negative interaction as the paper explains.

"Mark, what did you take from what Lucy just said?"

"Not much."

"Not much? In my paper it talks about understanding. Would you be able to show Lucy that you understood her?"

"Lucy says she doesn't get angry, but she does."

"Mark, you just dismissed the information Lucy was trying to tell you. Would you try it again with understanding only and no judgment?"

Mark rolled his eyes and then began. "Lucy said she doesn't get angry, but she criticizes and stonewalls me and, to tell you the truth, I'm sick of it. We came here to fix Lucy's anger problems, and now I get accused of dismissing her."

"Correct me if I'm wrong, but I thought you came here to find out if you could strengthen your relationship."

"You're right. I'm sorry. I'm just frustrated. I try to do everything for her and agree to marry her, and then she stonewalls me all week."

"Lucy, you said earlier that you stonewalled Mark. Why would you stonewall your boyfriend?"

"I did a lot of thinking this week," I began. "Coming to therapy, reading these papers, it got me thinking. I criticize too much, but why do I criticize? I want a man to make me feel special. I don't ask for a lot. I feel special when Mark says he'll pick me up at a certain time and actually comes at that time. I feel special when he thinks about a date for us instead of just coming over to watch my color TV. I would feel special if he brought me a little gift or did something to show he cares. I don't feel special in this relationship. I do use thinking strategies, but I don't throw good passes. I'm willing to try, but I don't think it'll work. I've given up and gone on to being one of these mean girlfriends who just criticizes."

"Mark?"

"I've given up trying to make Lucy feel special. She doesn't seem to appreciate anything I do."

"If this week could be a good week, Mark, what would it look like?"

"I would get to see Lucy four times, and we would smile and enjoy each other."

"Lucy?"

"I want the week free of seeing Mark. I think we got into some bad habits, and we have to figure out if we're willing to work on the things you have taught us. Mark just said he wanted to see me four times. He dismissed what I said about dates. If he comes over four times, he will eat me out of house and home and watch the Sox."

"Lucy, I would like to see you on Wednesday and take you to Uno Pizzeria."

"That'd be great. What time should I expect you?"

"I will be at your apartment at 6:30."

"See you then."

"Very good," said Dr. Stone with a nod. "I hope you'll work on some of the things we discussed. Let's meet again next Monday and see how you're doing."

On Wednesday, Mark came to my apartment at 6:24, six minutes early.

"Hi, Mark, it's good to see you. How was your day?"

"How was my day? I made it by six-thirty. Aren't you thrilled?"

"I'm happy that you came when you said you would, but I'm not happy about you expecting me to be thrilled because you did this once and probably only because we have to report back to

Dr. Stone. I want you to want to be with me. I want today to be positive."

"Luce, come on. Lighten up a little."

"Lighten up? Didn't you read the relationship paper? You just dismissed me again. You signed up for this couples counseling because you thought you could turn me into what you wanted. You can't. I'm me. You've made no effort to use the information Dr. Stone has given us to try to help us so that we can be happy. Is everything just a joke to you?"

"Fine. Let's just go."

"Let's just go? You again made no effort to understand what I just said. I don't want to go. Would you please just leave?"

"If I leave, and we don't go to get pizza, I'm ending this. I'm going to find someone who appreciates me for who I am."

"Great! Would you please just go?" I said. I started to tear up but just looked at him sternly.

Mark shook his head and rolled his eyes. He then turned around and walked out the door.

I just sat there for a minute and thought about it. I had invested a lot into this relationship, but I just couldn't get over him not putting in any effort since we started counseling. One part of the communications paper hit me—about how someone who thinks negatively before the situation has occurred will find a way to make it a negative experience. I tried to go into today with a clean slate. I was thinking positively about tonight. But it was just a joke to Mark to come early.

I called my friend Katie and talked to her a while. I explained what had happened, and she just listened. She didn't pass judgment. She didn't say she'd warned me that Mark was not a good fit.

She also didn't say he was a good man and I should call him. She just listened to me process.

I didn't see or hear from Mark the rest of the week. I tried to keep busy with writing, running and visiting friends. I did think about him on Friday because of the news of a passenger train crash in France that killed 108 people. Although this happened across the Atlantic, I knew the tragedy would take a toll on his day.

I got a call from him on Sunday evening.

"Hi. How are you?" he said.

"I'm doing okay. I've come to grips with the fact I no longer have a boyfriend."

"Why would you say that? We've been through these things before."

"No, we haven't. You said you were ending this. My father taught me to take what I'm given. I took it that you meant it. We're no longer together. After you didn't listen to me, I'm now trying to decide if I still want you as a friend."

"I listened to you. No, I didn't reflect back like the paper says, but I listened."

"Wow, you did read the paper! When did you read it?"

"What's it matter? Fine, I read it this morning. You're the girl of my dreams! I want to work this out."

"I'm sorry. We broke up. I want some time off. This has been too negative for me, and I've become a mean, critical person. I want to find myself again and figure out what I want. Would you give me some time, please?"

"How much time?"

"I want two months."

"You want the entire summer? What are we going to do about our appointment tomorrow?"

"We have an appointment, so I'm going. I want to tell Dr. Stone what we've decided to do. You have the appointment too. You can come if you want."

"Do you want me to come?"

"No, I want a couple months of not talking to you. We broke up. But I can't stop you if you want to come."

The next day I sat in the waiting area. There was no sign of Mark.

When Dr. Stone came out and looked at me, she said, "Is Mark running late?"

"We broke up." I told her the story of Wednesday night and our conversation on Sunday.

At about twenty minutes past the hour, there was a knock at the door. It was Mark. Dr. Stone asked me if it would be okay if he joined us, and I agreed.

I just looked at him with sad eyes. I didn't say anything about him being late.

"Mark, how'd the week go for you?"

"Well, I'm sure Lucy already told you the story. She has decided to dump me and not give me a chance."

"Lucy did tell me about her week. You believe she dumped you? Why don't you tell me about Wednesday?"

"I got there early. I tried to please her. She didn't say anything about me being on time.

Instead of appreciating my effort, I could tell she expected it."

"We established in our last session that you would be there by six-thirty. I thought that was everyone's expectation," said Dr. Stone.

"She then decided she didn't want to go to the restaurant after I made this effort. I'm just sick of her doing this to me. I told her if she didn't go, I would end it."

"So you broke up with her because she didn't want to go?"

"Yeah, but I called back on Sunday."

"Lucy has requested to go ahead with the break and doesn't want you to contact her. She told me she's not ruling out reconciliation but wants the summer to think about it. I think this is a good idea. It seems there has been a lot of damage, and if the two of you do decide to date again, you really need to put the past aside and give each other a clean slate. In my paper, I talk about the 30-Day Rule, which means you shouldn't bring up negative things that occurred more than 30 days ago because when you do, it's usually only to hurt the other person. If you decide to try again, you'll need to go into it without negative thinking. You'll need to go in thinking about how you want to love and support each other. You'll also want to understand, accept and appreciate the other person. Whether you get back together or if you decide to date others, I hope you'll consider these things. And if you decide you want help from me in the future, just call me. Thank you. It was nice meeting both of you."

"I want to live.
I want to give.
I've been a minor for a heart of gold."
— Neil Young (1972)

Giant Wheel

My mother told me that my cousin Rod had enlisted in the Air Force and would be in for four years. She said he had a low draft-lottery number and wanted to avoid being drafted and sent to Vietnam. By enlisting, he was hopefully going to stay in the US and start taking classes at night toward his degree.

This got me thinking. He wouldn't get to continue with his dream of being a rock drummer. I also thought about him having to cut his long hair. I really hoped he wouldn't get killed in war or go to Vietnam.

Then this morning, only a couple weeks after Rod had enrolled, President Nixon announced that no new troops would be sent to Vietnam. Had Rod made the right decision? If he'd known this was going to happen, would he have enlisted? He could have waited and, if he got drafted, spent only two years in the army, maybe without leaving the US.

I feared what would happen if Nixon didn't get re-elected this year and I got drafted in four years. What decision would I make? Even though I couldn't vote, I decided I was going to support Nixon's re-election to keep me safe from being killed at war. I didn't know at the time that this was a political maneuver to raise his chances of re-election. It worked on me.

A little while later, as I worked the morning shift at Gramps', a couple of very strong-looking guys walked up to rent a boat. One was very tall with a large frame, and the other was smaller and more tanned, but he just looked strong.

"Hey, man, could we get a row boat?"

"Sure," I said and went on to tell them about the prices. "You guys play for the Lions?" I asked.

They both smiled and laughed. The smaller guy said, "Someday we hope to. I'm George, George of the Jungle and this is my buddy, Ape. We play on the Wayne State football team. I play safety and Ape plays defensive tackle."

I was amazed. I had real college football players talking to me.

Finally the bigger guy said, "My name's George too, but George calls me Ape from the *George of the Jungle* cartoon."

We all laughed. It was so much fun talking to these guys. What a great job this was!

"Let's get two boats," George of the Jungle added. "I want to see who can row faster, me or Ape."

I got them each a cushion and pushed them out. They could row those boats faster than anyone I had seen. I wanted to row like these guys.

About 1 pm Teresa came with her friend Shelly and brought me a sandwich.

"Hungry, my boyfriend machine?"

"I'm always hungry, T. Hey, Shel."

"Hey, Tom."

As we ate, I told her about the Georges and about Rod.

"Shelley and I have been working on our swimming. We came down to Gramps' early this morning and swam to his raft and back twice without stopping."

"Oh, man, I want to do that," I told her.

"I had to work my way up to it. Two days ago, I swam to the raft and stopped. Yesterday, I swam there and back, and today I did it twice."

"I'll give it a try later."

"Where's Stan today?"

"He'll be here soon."

Almost on command, Stan rode up on his bike. "Hey!" he called.

"Shelley, this is Stan the Man!" I said.

Stan blushed but then said, "Hey!"

"Let's play some Frisbee," said Shelley.

We all tossed the Frisbee around. Stan was pretty shy, so we expected little out of him, but he actually made an effort to talk to Shelley. They both smiled a lot and appeared to like each other.

"So, Shelley, how long are you staying with Teresa's grandparents?" asked Stan.

"I don't know. This is great out here by the lake. It's a lot better than being at home with my parents yelling at each other."

There was a silence, and then Teresa said, "There must be something in the air. My mother is leaving my stepfather, but I'm happy about it. And I got to come out here for the summer. But the bad part is that I don't know where I'll live or go to school in the fall."

"That's what I'm wondering too," responded Shelley.

I looked at Stan, and finally he said, "I guess I'll join the crowd. My parents are talking about a divorce too, but I really don't want to move."

As I heard the conversation between the three of them, I reflected on my own situation. I hadn't been faced with the breakup of my parents because my mother never married. Is it possible that I was the lucky one, even though I didn't have a garage and nice houses like them?

I could see Stan starting to bond with Shelley over the unknown of their parents' situations. They continued to talk about it as I saw Bernie walking up. I knew he'd taken my mother out on his boat and had gone out with her a few times as well. I'd heard her talking on the phone about him, even though she refers to him as Guy.

"Hey, Tom, you working? I'm looking to pull some skiers."

"Hi. I know it doesn't look like it, but I am working," I said with a laugh.

"Man, I gotta get a job like you."

"It's not that busy. Why don't you and Stan go out? I'll cover for you," said Teresa.

"Wow! Thanks!"

So Stan and I took turns skiing with Bernie. We had fun showing the girls our sprays and joking around with him. I really liked him, and I knew my mom did too. Could he be my stepdad someday? That would be great, except that he lived far away in Dearborn and had a great job at Ford. I really just wanted to get through the next four years at Walled Lake Central and not move. He also had children. I'm not so sure about a brother and sister.

When we got done skiing, we thanked Bernie.

"Your mother and I were talking about getting Little Caesar's later," he said. "How 'bout we bring it down here and everyone can have some?"

Teresa and Shelley went home to ask her mother while I manned the boat docks. They came back a little later and told me they had cleared it.

Not long after that, my mother and Bernie came back with the 'za. It was delicious. Little Caesar's pizza was probably my absolute favorite food, and Bernie liked it too. I started imagining my mother with him and how we could get 'za several times a week.

Later we played horseshoes. Stan and I took on Bernie and my mother. I was surprised that my mother was actually better than I thought she'd be. I figured she couldn't throw the shoe all the way to stake, but she did. Bernie was pretty good too. However, I was tough to beat because I practiced every day, and Stan and I won both games.

My mother sure seemed happy to be around Bernie. He was very positive with me, unlike one of her previous boyfriends, and Bernie told us he would take us all to Cedar Point, a big amusement park in Ohio.

All was good with Teresa too. This summer was one of the best. The weird thing was that I was spending the time at the lake working, not playing baseball.

After a while, Bernie took my mother out in the boat, and they stayed out for over an hour. Stan stayed into the evening because I think he really liked Shelley. We laughed and had a good time and hopefully at least for a little while, everyone's minds were off their parents' situations.

— ✦ —

The next day I started practicing my swimming and followed Teresa's plan. The first day I was able to swim to Gramps' raft. The next day, I swam and touched it and swam back. I kept this up every day that it wasn't raining until I could swim there ten times and back without stopping.

I originally did this so that if any kind of emergency ever happened out on the lake, I could be confident I could swim to shore. What I hadn't planned on was my shoulders and arms getting harder. I felt myself getting stronger.

Last year, for eighth-grade football, I was the starting quarterback, just like Coach Skinner had said I'd be. But he had so many guys that I only played on offense and didn't get in on defense. We ran the blast play pretty much every time, so I was nothing more than someone who handed the ball off. I only had eleven passes all year, and they were all very short. I only got to run the ball fourteen times, and most were quarterback sneaks. Most kids probably would be happy to be the starting quarterback, but I really missed playing defensive end. I was growing taller and getting stronger, and this year I was determined get back on the defensive side of the ball.

As I felt myself get stronger, I also started doing pushups every day, and my chest started to look like a football player's chest. One day Stan looked at me and told me I was really looking strong. He wondered how I was doing it. So Stan started doing pushups and swimming too. When I told him rowing helped with strength too, he started rowing as well.

—◆—

I went down to the docks for work, Teresa and Shelley were laying out in their bikinis. I went and sat on the picnic table, hoping not to disturb them, but they soon realized my presence.

"Didn't want to disturb you while you were working," I told them.

Teresa smiled. "Yes, we're working on our tans. What do you think?"

"Well, Gramps tried to tell me I was the sun of the beach, but clearly you and Shelley are the sun, the moon and the stars."

"It was so nice of Bernie to include us in the Cedar Point trip. We're going this weekend, right? Who's going to cover the docks?"

"Gramps told me his grandson Todd would be working, but I think he'll be here with Mollie's entire family. Gramps just wanted to remind us that a nine-year-old could do the job."

On Saturday Bernie, his son Carl, his daughter Karen, my mom, Stan, Teresa, Shelley and I all loaded up in two cars and traveled down to Ohio to go to Cedar Point. I agreed to ride with Bernie and his children while my mom headed off with the other 14-year-olds. I never liked amusement parks, and I knew my mother didn't either. She referred to them as paying money to have a bad time, and I agreed. It just didn't make sense to me to get on rides to be terrified.

Unfortunately, the rides didn't seem to bother Teresa and Shelley. They'd get on anything. I tried to pretend I was being polite and told them to have fun on the rides while I watched our stuff.

Then we came to the new attraction, which would become the picture of Cedar Point: the Giant Wheel. Cedar Point had wanted to build a Ferris wheel bigger than all others.

"Oh, Tom, we have to try the Giant Wheel. It'll be so romantic," Teresa told me.

I looked at her for a minute and then looked up at how high it was. I couldn't really imagine going up in it.

"Let's go get in line," she said.

I looked into her eyes and saw everything I wanted in a girlfriend. Then I looked at the line, which was long. What could it hurt to go stand in line?

As we got farther up in the line toward the Giant Wheel, I began to think about how Gramps had told me to approach dental visits. This was just another chair I had to sit in for a brief amount of time and endure the pain. I'd been to the dentist several times. Why couldn't I stand this ride if I could stand the dental chair?

I finally decided it'd go better if I just acted happy. I really wanted it to be fun for Teresa. So when it came time for us to get in the seat, I walked right toward it, holding Teresa's hand and smiling.

They locked the safety bar behind us, and we were off. Because they were still loading the other seats, it took some time for us to get higher.

"Isn't this a magnificent view? We can see the whole park," she said.

I held her hand with my right hand but hung on for dear life with my left arm. "Wow, what a great view," I said, even though I didn't care about the view. I just couldn't wait to get off.

"You're not scared, are you?"

"I've never been on this ride before, so I might have some *opening day jitters*, that's all.

Finally, the ride stopped, and we got off. I wanted to kiss the ground, letting it know I was happy to be back, but I just smiled at Teresa, and we walked off to explore the park some more.

At the end of the day, we packed up to go home. To make the cars four and four, I again agreed to ride with Bernie and his kids. But this ride was quite different than the ride to the park. The kids were really fussy because they must've been tired after a long day. I had to listen to them whine and listen to Bernie trying to soothe them.

I really liked Bernie, and it was great that he liked my mom so much, but if they ever got married, my idea of a quiet house would go away.

"Bernie, I've got an idea. Would you mind if I sang to them?"

"No, please."

I decided to start with one of my favorite songs. "*And the sign said long-haired freaky people need not apply, so I tucked my hair up under my hat and I went in to ask him why...*"

When I started singing, the kids stopped fussing. After the song ended, they got a little restless again, so I decided to try an Eddie Arnold song called, "That's How Much I Love You." It had five verses, but they really got a kick out of the third verse, which was, "*Now if you were a horsefly and I an old grey mare, I'd stand and let you bite me and never move a hair.*"

Not long after that both the children fell asleep, and Bernie and I talked the rest of trip. Whenever I saw the kids after that, they would ask me to sing "long-haired freaky people" and the "horsefly song."

The next day, Bernie and Charlie came out to the docks and put up a basketball hoop bordering the parking lot. This place was becoming more and more fun. I got a lot of practice shooting baskets after that.

"You know I love the ladies.
Love to have my fun.
I'm a high night flyer and a rainbow rider,
A straight shootin' son of gun."
— Three Dog Night (1971)

Roger Dodger

The day after our therapy session I got up to go to work. Just before I left, I remembered I was supposed to give Louise a kiss. I went into the bedroom and saw her lying on her side. I put my hand on her back as I sat on the bed and bent down to kiss her on the cheek, hoping she didn't wake up.

I saw her smile and she said softly, "Thanks, honey. Have a good day at work."

As I drove to my job, I thought about her. I hadn't seen her smile like that in a long time. I thought about her several more times throughout the day, but I also thought about other ladies. After a few more couples sessions, I would be free to roam and find a younger woman.

When I got home and walked in the door, Louise ran to hug me and ask about my day. It felt great to have her hugging me and smiling. I thought about making some comment about therapy, but I decided to just go with it.

"How was your day, dear?" she said.

"Just the typical day at the plant," I told her.

"I made you your favorite meal, with Polish sausage."

"Great. Where's Stan?"

"Stan's over at Gramps' Docks with Tom."

"Well, let's eat."

I went into the kitchen and picked up my plate to carry it into the living room to watch TV while I ate.

"Would you mind eating at the table tonight?" Louise asked. "We could get our five minutes of talking in while we eat."

I took a deep breath and set my plate back down on the table. We began to eat.

"I really appreciated you kissing me before you left for work today," she said.

"It was nothing."

"Well, it was something to me. I had a good day. I got a lot done."

"Oh, what'd ya get done?"

"I got the basement organized and have a lot of things we can sell in the garage sale."

"After I eat, I'd like to see what you did. Ah, I'm supposed to ask you on a date. Do you want to watch the fireworks with me down at the neighborhood beach on the Fourth of July?"

"That's your date? We always watch the fireworks on the Fourth. How original!"

"I figured that would be the thanks I got for trying to make the effort." I scowled.

"I do appreciate your effort. I would also be interested in going out to dinner this weekend. It doesn't need to be anything too fancy. I'd be happy to go to Big Boy. But just you and me."

"Fine. Does Saturday work? I haven't had a good Slim Jim in a long time."

We finished eating, and I believe I satisfied the five minutes. Then we went down the basement.

"Where's the stuff for the garage sale?" I asked.

"It's all right here."

"What? My old baseball glove?"

"You don't use it."

"No, I don't but it has sentimental value. I almost made it to the bigs with this glove. And we're certainly not getting rid of any of my old jerseys. These mean a lot to me."

"I know. All of this stuff means a lot more to you than I do. You won't throw this out, but you're ready to discard me."

She stormed off up the stairs. She was right. I was certainly ready for a new girlfriend, but I wouldn't give up my stuff.

We didn't follow through on the greetings and the five-minute talks the rest of the week, but when it was Saturday, Louise reminded me about our Big Boy date.

"You're taking me to Big Boy tonight, right?"

Stan overheard this and commented that he wanted to go. I looked at Louise to see what she would say.

"Stan, this is supposed to be my date with your father for the week."

"Date? What? You're married! I want to go to Big Boy!"

"Your father and I have agreed to a date once a week to try to improve our marriage."

"I'm all for that. I have an idea. Let's all go to Big Boy and then you can drop me off at the docks to hang with Tom while the two of you go to the Commerce Drive-In."

"Good idea, Stan. You're such a bright young man. Roger?"

"I really don't want to go to the drive-in. I'll tell you what, we can all go to Big Boy, and then you and I can take a stroll to the beach and look at the stars, Louise."

So we all went to Big Boy, and as we were eating, four younger ladies sat down—all wearing midriff tops, shorts and flip flops. I certainly got distracted and started thinking about how good they looked.

After dinner, we dropped Stan off and headed home. Louise went in the bedroom and came out wearing a midriff top, shorts and flip flops.

"Hey, whatcha doing? It's going to be a little chilly on our walk."

"Obviously this is what you like. You couldn't take your eyes off those ladies at the restaurant."

"What?"

"Come on. I saw you staring at those girls."

"I only looked at them because I thought they might be cold," I said, trying to recover. I couldn't figure out what Louise's problem was. All guys look at girls, especially those half-dressed.

"I'm ready to go if you want to follow through on our date."

We walked to the beach. She reached down and held my hand. I thought I'd better let her do this or I'd hear about it in therapy. We sat on a picnic table at the beach, and I pointed out some of the constellations.

"Where's Cupid?" she asked.

"Oh, I don't think Cupid is a constellation."

"I'm disappointed that there isn't a love constellation," she said as she touched my face and kissed me on the lips.

We walked back and watched TV while waiting for Stan to get home.

— ✦ —

The next Thursday, we attended our appointment with Dr. Stone.

"It's so good to see the two of you," she said. "Tell me about the positives from the week."

I decided I should speak first. "We accomplished everything. We greeted in the morning. We greeted when I got home from work. We talked for five minutes. We went on a romantic date. And I saved my classic baseball jerseys from a garage sale," I said, giving a big smile on the last item.

"It sounds like a lot of positives. Louise?"

"You just got the sugar-coated version. Yes, we did the greetings and the five-minute talk the first day after leaving the session but not the other days. The date didn't work out well. We took our son with us, and Roger gaped at half-bare-naked ladies."

"Louise, was this past week better than previous weeks?"

"It was about the same for me, except that Roger tried to satisfy your requirements so he could come here and tell you how well he did."

"So, Louise, it sounds like we really didn't make any improvement. What must happen this week so that it's better?"

Louise started to cry. "I just want to be loved, and he doesn't do anything to show that he loves me."

I decided I should pat her back to show some love, but it backfired because she said, "See? This is Roger's absolute best attempt at love. I want him to tell me how beautiful I am. I want him to smile when sees me. I want him to not be able to take his eyes off me. I'm sick of him looking at every lady in town and not me. I want a man who at least likes to be with me."

"Louise, can we name a few specific things you want Roger to do this week?"

"Yes, I want him to get out and leave me alone. I want a divorce so I can have a real man. If he wants to go chase panties, let him. I want a relationship with someone who only wants me."

I knew Louise was upset, but I wasn't sure if she really meant what she was saying.

"Roger, what is Louise trying to tell you?"

"I heard her say I'm not good enough, and she wants another man. Fine. I don't have to put up with this. But I don't know where to go."

Louise wiped her tears and said, "I talked to my parents, and Stan and I can go to Indiana for three weeks and stay with them. It'll give us three weeks to figure out what we want."

I didn't know what to say. I knew Stan had finished baseball and three weeks would bring him back before he needed to start football. And this would give me three weeks to date who I wanted and not be bothered by Louise.

"If that's what you want, I want you to be happy," I told her.

"Roger, what're you going to do during the three weeks?" asked Dr. Stone.

"Well, the first two weeks I'll work, but the third week is changeover at work, and I have the week off."

"Do you plan on talking to each other during the time you're in Indianapolis?" asked Dr. Stone.

"I really don't know. I think we need the time apart," said Louise.

"I would at least like to hear from Stan once a week while you're gone," I told her.

"Fine. I'll have Stan call you."

"Could we schedule an appointment when you get back to see how we want to proceed?" asked Dr. Stone.

We all agreed.

Since I had some freedom for three weeks, I decided to call Tom's mom to see if she wanted to go for a boat ride.

"Eve, this is Roger—ah, you know, Tom's coach."

"Hi, Coach. Tom's not home right now. Could I take a message?"

"Ah, um, I was actually going to take my boat out and wondered if you wanted to go for a ride."

"I thought Louise was out of state?"

"Louise and I have separated."

"So it would just be you and me? Sorry, Coach. It would be wrong for you and me to be alone together."

Well, that didn't go well. I decided to try another lady.

"Hi, Connie. This is Roger."

"Roger, how've you been? It's been a long time. I got married last month."

"Wow, that's great news. I hadn't heard. Congratulations!"

"Oh no, you weren't calling to ask me out, were you? You're a day late and dollar short. Good hearing from you though."

Strike two on two very attractive ladies. But I'm not going to strike out. In baseball, when you get two strikes, you choke up on the bat a little and try to get a base hit instead of a homerun. This was exactly what I planned do. This lady at work really wasn't very attractive, but she flirted with me a lot.

The next day at work, I saw her. "Hey, Betsy, how are you?"

"I'm doing great, you big hunk of a man. Want to go to the bar after work?"

This was a piece of cake. "Actually, sure. I'm free. Are you stopping at Dusty's?"

"I'll be there. Can't wait."

I stopped at Dusty's, and Betsy had changed from her work clothes into a very low-cut top and short skirt. I approached her and ordered a drink.

She talked and talked, and it was as if she'd waited all week to talk to someone. Her voice was so loud it started to hurt my eardrums. The more she talked, the more obnoxious I found her. She just seemed so excited to be talking to me.

"Are you ready to take me home yet? I've wanted to be with you for some time," she told me. "I've been waiting to get together. Let's go to my place."

Here was my chance to get my base hit, but she was just too obnoxious. "Now, Betsy, you know I'm married. I have to get home to my wife," I said.

"Hey, she'll just think you're out with the guys. Do you want me?" she said with a big smile.

"I'm sorry. I have to go."

I paid the bill and left. Strike three. I got home and actually started missing Louise some. At least she wasn't loud.

I spent the next few weeks just relaxing and getting things done around the house. After striking out, I needed a break.

Tough Customers

On Monday, I had the morning shift, and it was quiet for a while. I was practicing shooting baskets into Gramps' new net when three rather overweight ladies showed up and asked about renting a boat.

"Come on, I want my own. I'm not riding with you two," said a lady dressed in yellow.

"Pay for it yourself then," said the lady dressed in red with her belly hanging out.

"I'm not paying. It was your idea," said the third woman, who wore purple.

"Then we're all going together."

"May I help you, ma'am?" I asked.

"Who you callin' ma'am? How old do you think I am?" said the lady in red.

"I'm sorry. Would you like to rent a boat?" I asked.

"I don't have a clue how to row a boat. I figure we could handle a canoe though. How much?"

"You want one canoe for all three of you?" The ladies nodded yes.

"How long do you want it?"

"One hour will be plenty long enough."

"Okay. That'll be three dollars." I finished checking them in and got them their life cushions.

They continued to argue with each other about who would be sitting in which spot, but finally the lady in red took the back, the lady in purple took the middle, and the lady in yellow took the front. I helped shove them off and listened as they continued to yell at each other and call each other names.

They hadn't gotten too far out when I saw the lady in the middle stand up. The canoe started to wobble.

"Sit your fat rear down," said the lady in red.

But it was too late. The entire canoe tipped over. My first instinct was to run off the end of the dock and swim to help them. I then quickly decided to throw about five life cushions in a boat and row toward them.

When I got there, two of the ladies were holding on to the canoe but the other was yelling help and having a hard time staying above water. I rowed close to her and threw her a life cushion.

"Grab it!" I yelled.

She tried but couldn't. So I rowed right next to her and handed her a cushion. I then maneuvered the boat so she could grab on to the back. She was coughing water but able to hang on. I then asked the other ladies to grab the back of the boat as well.

"What about the canoe?"

"I'll come back for it," I told them. "If all three of you would grab the back of the boat, I want to get you to shore safely. Once you're safe, I'll come back for the canoe."

They all grabbed the back, still jawing at one another about who'd caused the accident. I had to row with everything I had given there was likely more than six hundred pounds on the back of the boat. It took much longer than usual to row to the boat launch.

I got the ladies to shore and asked the one who'd been coughing if she was okay or needed to go to the hospital. She told me she would be okay. I asked the ladies to wait there and rowed out to get the canoe. After I'd collected the cushions and paddles, I towed it to the boat launch. I pulled it up and emptied the water. Then I took all of the wet cushions and put them in the sun to dry.

I went back over and reluctantly asked the ladies if they would like to try again.

"I'm not going back out there," said the lady in purple who had been coughing.

The other two ladies wanted another chance, so I got them two dry cushions.

"Please don't stand up this time, and try to work cooperatively," I said.

The lady gave me a dirty look and said, "This kid must think he's Einstein. Don't worry about us."

I felt like saying something back, but I remembered that she was the customer, and I had to put up with her.

As they headed off, the lady left behind approached me.

"What's your name?'

"Tom."

"Tom, I'm sorry my friends are so rude. You saved my life. I might have drowned. Is there anything I can do for you?" She smiled really big.

"I just did my job. I'm happy you're all okay." I didn't smile, hoping she would leave me alone. "I just want to keep an eye on your friends to make sure they don't capsize again."

When the other two ladies came in, they pulled up to the boat ramp yelling at each other. Then they commented about how the canoes weren't safe here, and the lady in purple started arguing that she wouldn't be here if it weren't for me.

I was glad when they finally left, but I felt stressed for the rest of my shift and wondered what I would've done if I'd rowed out to the ladies and found one of them underwater.

Teresa arrived about half an hour before she had to start. We had been bringing each other lunch, but she didn't have anything with her today.

"I'm starving," I said. "It was a rough day."

"Oh, did you have to rent a boat today?"

"Never mind with that attitude."

"You're the one complaining that I didn't bring you lunch."

"I didn't say that."

"You did. Listen to yourself once in a while. Why are all these cushions wet?"

I didn't respond and just stopped talking to her. She didn't even care that I'd saved a lady's life. I just kept to myself until it was time to leave.

"Tom, I wish you'd talk to me."

"I'd like to, but I'm really hungry. I'll see ya tomorrow." I walked home to get something to eat. I really was hungry.

After finding some lunch, I decided to walk down to Gramps' house and hoped he would be there. But when I got there I didn't see him out, so I sat on the picnic table.

It wasn't too long later when I heard a familiar sound. "Tommy Boy," he called.

I smiled and turned to see Gramps.

"How's my hard worker doing?"

"It was a tough day. Three ladies came to rent a canoe, and they tipped over."

"Are they okay?"

"I grabbed as many cushions as I could and rowed a boat out to them. One lady looked like she was ready to go under, so went to her first and got her to hang on to the back of the boat."

"Good job, Tom."

"I then got the other ladies to hang on to the back of the boat and rowed them in."

I waited for Gramps to ask about the canoe, but he didn't.

"Tom, you acted just like I thought you would. You saved a lady from a possible drowning. I'm really proud of you."

"After they were safe, I went out and collected the paddles, cushions and canoes."

"As soon as you turn fifteen, you should get your lifesaving certificate. Of course, then I might have to pay you more," he said with a smile.

"I also had an argument with Teresa, and we didn't leave on good terms."

"You really like her, don't you?"

"I really like her, but then there are days like today, and I start to wonder."

"My good friend Dr. Stone wrote a paper on relationships. Would you like to read it?"

"I guess I need it."

"We all do. I never kept a girlfriend for even two months when I was your age. I'll get it for you before you leave. Read the section on understanding and the section on repair. Then let me know what you think. I'm heading over to help Teresa wash the boats around eight-thirty this evening."

"I'll read those sections. I really do like her."

Gramps gave me the paper, and I went home and read.

Knowing Gramps would be heading down at 8:30, I decided to go see Teresa at 7:00 to try to repair our relationship and understand her. The paper Gramps gave me had talked about throwing the best pass I could if my goal was to repair things, as bad passes don't help win games. This Dr. Stone spoke my language. Before I left, I'd asked my mother if I could take her some brownies, my peace offering.

"Hi, Teresa."

"Hey, Tom."

"I brought you some brownies."

"Oh, thanks."

"I don't think I've been a good boyfriend to you, but I want to really listen and see what we can do to get our relationship back on track."

"Tom, you're you. You're the sweetest and best-looking guy I have ever met. I just wasn't happy that you didn't thank me for lunch on Saturday."

"I didn't?" She just looked at me. "Oh, I'm sorry. I should have. I guess I forgot. I may forget again even though I'm sure I do feel grateful. Do me a favor? If I forget, ask how I liked my lunch?"

Teresa smiled. "That's fair. But there's something else I've been upset about. You told me to wait a month to see if we were still girlfriend/boyfriend before you would kiss me. Do you know how long ago that was?"

"I'm not sure, but I know it's been longer than a month."

"I'm starting to think you don't find me attractive and don't want me as your girlfriend."

"What? You know that's not true."

"Then what is it?"

I shut my eyes for about ten seconds and then said, "I'm not really sure. You're the prettiest girl I've ever met. I guess I think that if I'm kissing you, I'm just using you for pleasure. I care for you. I don't want to do that."

"Oh, Tom. You're so sweet. I don't think there's anything wrong with two fourteen year olds kissing, hugging and holding hands. I really want this with you, and only you. I want this to be just between us."

"We kissed four years ago. I guess I'm worried you won't like the way I kiss," I told her.

"Oh, Tom. It was so sweet when you kissed me four years ago. I knew you really liked me. If we kiss again, it'll be awkward for both of us. I don't know if you'll like my kiss." We just looked at each other for a minute and then she continued, "I'll wait until you're ready."

I walked over and put my arms around her. I looked into those big eyes and said, "I'm ready now." I put my lips against hers and held them there for about ten seconds and then smacked. I repeated this several times. Each time my lips touched hers I felt powerless and knew that this was the best feeling in the world.

"Wow!" said Teresa. "You're a great kisser."

I breathed a few times. "There's no better feeling than kissing you."

"Thanks for coming down tonight. I was hoping you would. Not many boys would make this effort to make up. How are you so smart?"

"I must admit I get help from Gramps. He gave me a paper to read on relationships, and it's helping me. I don't want to lose you."

"What? A paper? Can I read it too?"

"Sure."

We sat on the picnic table together. I put my arm around her, and we waited for Gramps to come and clean the boats. And I told her the story of the three ladies renting a canoe.

Later that week I was working the morning shift when one of the Georges, the one the other referred to as Ape, walked up carrying an inner tube with an orange flag attached to it.

"Hey, George."

"Tom, man, you get stronger every time I see you. You'll be playing for Wayne State someday!"

I smiled.

"I'm going out to do some snorkeling—I want to see what kind of fish are in this lake. I've got my tube, so I don't need a boat."

"Sounds good. Have fun!"

A little while later, George came back in by the boat ramp. When he took off his mask, he really looked mad. What had I done?

"Did you see those speed boats out there?" George said practically screaming. "That white boat almost hit me. I could've been killed. What's wrong with these boat owners?" He got louder and louder. "I COULD'VE BEEN KILLED! I COULD'VE BEEN KILLED!"

George grabbed his tube and stomped off to his car. I could still hear him saying, "I could have been killed!"

I felt bad. I knew he wasn't mad at me, but he was really mad. I thought about Gramps' one-to-ten anger scale. Given that this was potentially a dangerous situation, it was probably a nine. *A nine.* Gramps had told me that if a situation's dangerous, it's okay to be angry. So I understood why George was so angry.

On August first, the news of the day was that the Democratic vice-presidential candidate had withdrawn from the race due to depression. This seemed so odd to me. How could someone that famous and successful be depressed? I thought about myself. Was I depressed? I didn't think so. I felt pretty happy.

A couple days later George Wallace, a candidate for president, was shot. He survived but would be wheelchair bound. Why would anyone want to shoot George Wallace? Richard Nixon was the incumbent, and he seemed like a shoe-in to get four more years.

I would've never guessed that after Nixon won by a landslide, he would have to resign before the end of his term due to the Watergate break-in. Nixon's resignation led to a few years of presidency by a man from Michigan: Gerald Ford.

Stan, Denny and Floyd came riding up on their bikes while I was working. I hadn't seen Stan in a month, and he was my best friend. Granted, this was mostly because he'd been out of town, but could he stay my best friend now that Teresa was my girlfriend? I had to figure this out.

"Stan the Man. You're back! How was Indy?" I asked him.

"Hey, Tom. It was pretty good, but I missed you and my other buddies."

"Hey, let's throw the football," said Denny. "We have to get ready for Walled Lake Central football. There's one-a-days next week."

We had fun throwing the football and joking around.

"I remember finding out about you.
Every day my mind is all around you.
Looking out of my lonely room, day after day."
— Badfinger (1971)

Labor Day Eve

I continued to go out with Guy throughout the
summer. Besides spending time on the boat,
he took me to movies, a Tiger game, Cedar
Point, and dinners. I've never felt so loved as I did
when he put his arms around me and held me. It
was magical.

Of course he lives forty minutes away and
works during the week, so I didn't get to see him as
much as I would've liked. Sometimes he would go
days without calling, and my thoughts ran wild.
Did he have another girlfriend? Why wasn't I good
enough for him? Was it my looks? Does he not
want to accept Tom? Does he not like the way I
interact with his kids? Does he want someone with
a degree? A better job?

Finally, this week I had once again waited
for days without hearing from him. What should I
do? Should I just let this go? Maybe I should find
an excuse to call him. Ah, a plan!

I rang his telephone.

"Guy? It's Eve. I have a question for you."

"Eve, aren't you watching the Tiger game?
It's really exciting. They're only down by one in the
ninth inning."

Here I thought I'd lost out to another
woman, and I was losing to a professional baseball
team.

"Can I ask you a question?"

"Would it be okay if I called you right when the game ends?" said Guy.

"This is an easy question. Do you think Tom and Teresa are too serious?"

"Eve, that's why you called me? I think Tom's just fine. He seems to be handling the relationship very maturely. Ah."

"What?"

"Kaline just struck out. He's playing past his prime. I just missed it. I didn't see if he was called out or if he struck out swinging."

"I have another question for you."

I could hear him sigh, but I couldn't take the chance that he wouldn't call me back. I had to think of another question quickly.

"Yes, what is it?" he said slowly.

"Oh, let me think?"

"Why are you doing this? You know I'm watching the game, and you're beating around the bush. Just tell me. Whatever it is, it'll be fine."

"Do you think I should wear dresses to work?"

"Shoot!"

"What happened?"

"If you were watching the game like everyone else in Michigan, you'd know. Freehan just flied out, and the Tigers lost. And no, you shouldn't wear dresses to your job. You should wear dresses with me."

"Well, I don't get to see you much."

"What? We just saw each other. We had a great time. Right?"

"It was four days ago. I don't think I'm what you want."

"Eve, I really like you a lot. Why are you saying this?

"Why haven't you asked me out again?

"I was going to come for Tom's first football game."

"Did you find some new young girl for this weekend?"

"No, the guys are having a party Saturday, so I'll be tied up."

"Can you bring a date?"

"It really isn't the type of party to bring dates."

"Oh, okay, just a guy's party." I bet he's having a singles party to see what kind of women he can meet.

"Would you mind if I stopped by Friday night? I want to pick up my coffee maker so I can have coffee this weekend."

I really was just looking for an excuse, and I didn't want any of his bimbos drinking coffee from my coffee maker.

"Um...sure," he said.

So I drove to Dearborn Friday night to get my coffee maker. When I arrived, I told Guy I wouldn't stay long because I knew he was busy.

"Eve. Wow! You look great! You wore the dress to work today?"

"I did, and a guy asked me out for tomorrow night."

He just looked at me. I could see he wasn't happy, but he didn't have a leg to stand on. I could see him looking at my legs. I got to him with the dress.

"Would you stay for dinner?" he asked.

"No, I have to get back."

He looked at me with those puppy dog eyes. "You look stunning."

It really felt good to hear him say that, and I wanted to jump into his arms and let him hold me tight, but I couldn't. I really wanted him to be my steady boyfriend. But he was still shopping around by having his party tomorrow. I needed someone who wanted me.

"Well, I better go. Hope your party goes well. I'm excited to have a date tomorrow. Maybe he'll want me."

"I want you."

"Well, you must not want me very badly." I got my coffee maker and drove back home crying much of the trip.

It was true that a man had asked me out for Saturday evening, but I declined. I told him I had a boyfriend. I just wanted to get Guy thinking, and it worked.

On Sunday morning, I got a call from Guy.

"Eve, I want to see you. What day is good?"

"How was the party? Did you meet any ladies you want to date?"

"Eve, look, I'm sorry. You were right!"

Oh, did I love hearing I was right.

"The summer's nearing an end, and I thought I might want to meet someone a little closer to home since I'll be pulling my boat soon."

"Well, did you find her?"

"No. You're so special to me. I really don't want to be with anyone but you. I don't care how far away you live. I have to support Ford by driving my truck, so I'd like to keep coming out to see you when I can. Did you like the man you went out with?"

"It didn't work out, so I stayed at home."

"I called you because I want to see you. Could we have dinner tonight?"

"I'd like that."

He came out and took me to John Cowley's restaurant in Farmington. I was still trying to get used to sit-down restaurants. I kept looking at him and thinking he was everything I want. Was he telling me the truth earlier? Was I what he wanted?

Near the end of the evening, Guy told me he planned to be out at the lake for all three days of the Labor Day weekend but would be pulling his boat out on that Monday. He told me his kids would be at their in-laws' for Sunday and Monday and wanted to know if I would spend Sunday with him on the boat. I agreed.

He called me three times during that week, and I'm sure he waited until the Tigers game was over because each time was late. But it was great to talk to him. I just didn't know what the future held. Would he really come see me after he pulled his boat out? Would he find his next romantic interest and pursue her? I wasn't sure, but I was determined to have a great day on Sunday with him.

When Sunday came, I walked to Gramps' docks to meet him. When I got there, he and Tom were shooting baskets at the basketball hoop.

"Hey, Mom. Bernie was just showing me some new moves," Tom told me.

"Bernie? It's Mr. Burns." I looked at Bernie.

"Eve, would it be okay if Tom calls me Bernie? It's not as formal."

"I don't like it."

"Mom, it's kinda like me calling Dr. Davis Gramps."

"Okay, fine. You want to be Bernie to my son? Be Bernie," I told Guy.

"Mom, watch this," Tom showed me one of the post-up moves Bernie had taught him.

"Looks good to me. But I thought you'd be getting ready for football."

"Basketball season is right after football, so I've been practicing both."

"Eve, have you ever seen your son water ski? He's really good."

"No, it seems so dangerous, but I know he does it. I'd guess I'd like to see him glide across the water."

Tom got excited and asked Gramps permission if he could be gone for twenty minutes. Tom came out in the boat with us. He told me good skiers use just one ski and get the best sprays.

I watched my son ski and was amazed that he could do it with such ease. I also watched how well he interacted with Guy. This had to be the first guy I've dated who Tom actually liked. And I liked Guy too. It was just complicated with his two children and him living so far away.

After a little while we dropped Tom off at the docks and headed back out. Guy and I had an amazing day. When I'm with him, I feel like a queen, but when we're apart I can't help but think that he will find someone else, and I won't hear from him again. I don't know how to fix this.

That night when I got back home there was a paper sitting on the couch. Tom must have been reading it. I picked it up and read: *Improving Relationships through Positive Interaction by Dr. Marjorie Stone.* My son never ceases to amaze me. I would expect some kind of sports magazine to study player statistics, but this? He must really care about Teresa. I decided to read the paper.

As I read each paragraph, I thought about how Guy and I were interacting. There was a section about knowing your partner and another about consistency. Guy was not good at checking in about how my day went, and there certainly wasn't a lot of consistency since I went days without hearing from him. But there was another paragraph about sharing fondness. This is where Guy excels. He certainly shows fondness for me when he's with me.

As I read on, I realized some areas where I might not be doing so well. The first one that jumped out at me was accepting Guy for who he is. I constantly want more of him, and why shouldn't I want more? Every moment we spend together is special. But I want to accept everything about him—like that he works, spends time with his children, and even that he watches sports on TV.

But the area of the paper that really got to me was the part about assuming your partner means well. I hadn't really thought about this until reading it. I assumed the negative all the time even though Guy was usually so good to me. Why did I do this? Was I defeating our relationship by assuming the negative? I really want to try to work on this.

—◆—

I decided not to call Guy this week and just accept him and assume he wants me. On Tuesday, he called to let me know that he had gotten off work for Tom's first high school football game. We talked, and I tried to use the techniques in Dr. Stone's paper. We agreed he would pick me up on Wednesday to go to the game.

He arrived as planned, and we enjoyed watching the game together. Tom was one of the biggest and best players, and he was so fun to watch. Many people commented on how well he was playing.

People are used to me sitting by myself during these games, so I wondered what they thought of Guy sitting next to me. I really hope they thought he was my boyfriend because he's so good looking and successful.

As we watched, Guy tried to tell me things about the game. "Did you see Tom stay home, read the play and not get caught in the backfield?" he would ask me. "He read that play so well." I didn't really know what he was talking about, but I could tell he was talking positively about Tom.

I know Guy would be a great father figure for Tom. They have such a bond, and they speak the same sports language. I wondered how I would do as a mother figure for his two children. I decided to tell Guy that I would like him to take Tom to a Lions game, and I would like to stay with Carl and Karen when they go.

After I explained this, I could see the excitement in his eyes. I could tell it was important to him that I get to know his children. He joked that he wanted to take Tom to the Lions game against the Dallas Cowboys in Dallas, but a few days later he told me he'd ended up getting tickets for the opening day game against the New York Giants in Detroit a week from Sunday.

On the day of their outing, I could tell Tom was excited about the game, and Guy was just like a kid when we arrived too. I was excited to spend the day with Carl and Karen.

Once Tom and Guy left, I started out having them show me all of their toys. They have a lot of them, and they gave me the grand tour. As they showed me the toys, they would stop and play with them for a while.

I made the peanut butter and jelly sandwiches for lunch, but it seemed like I'd taken them to a steak house because they were so excited to eat. My PB & Js must be better than Guy's. Just wait until they try my grilled cheese.

After a while they started to get a little restless, so I did what I knew best: singing. I started with "This Little Light of Mine." I held up my index finger as my light. Then I covered it up when singing "hide it under a bushel" and quickly moved uncovered it with an emphatic *No!*

Turns out Carl and Karen really liked the song, and it kept their attention for quite a while. I think they really liked the *No!* part. I tried other songs, and they liked them as well. We really had fun, and I noticed as we were singing that they'd both snuggled up close to me. Being a stepmother for these children was not going to be an obstacle in my relationship with Guy.

— ✦ —

A few weeks later I had a doctor's appointment—just a checkup. After the exam, my doctor said I was healthy, but there was a growth in my uterus she wanted to check further.

"Ms. Mochina, it's not uncommon for women to have benign growths, and I doubt this is anything, but I'd like you to schedule a test just to make sure it isn't cancerous."

"Cancer?"

"I really don't think it's cancer, but in case it is, we want to catch it early so we can maximize your options. Would it be okay if we get this test scheduled? This is just precautionary."

"Okay. I'll get the test done." My doctor was very nice, and I trusted her.

But how was I supposed to not worry about this? Cancer kills. Even though my doctor said she wasn't worried, I still wondered what would happen to Tom if I died.

Stepping Aside

I n mid-August, I talked to Gramps and he supported me playing football even though more practices meant I would have to leave my job.

"Who's going to rent the boats?" I asked.

"Teresa is staying for a little while longer, and I'll handle much of the other time. Mollie and Todd will help me. How's football going?"

"I've been playing both quarterback and defensive end so far during practices. Right now I'm starting both ways. I missed playing defensive end last year. I'm being challenged at quarterback by a new transfer to our school named Kenny who can really throw the ball and has good speed. He's much shorter than me, doesn't know the guys well but he had talent for the position."

"Get me a schedule! And Charlie will want one too."

"I really appreciate you giving me this job," I told Gramps. It's really worked out well for me, and I saved a lot of money too. Hopefully I can buy that Mercury Capri in a couple years."

"I can't wait to see you driving. How're things with Teresa?"

"Things have been great. We both read Dr. Stone's paper, and we're communicating really well. I'm really going to miss her."

"Miss her? Is she going somewhere?"

"Hmmm, I assumed she was going back. I'll ask her."

The next day I went to the docks after football, and Teresa was there.

"Hey," I said.

"Tom, good to see you. How's football?"

"Football's great! Hey, I've been wondering. Where are you going to live this fall?"

Teresa pulled out her guitar and started finger-picking a familiar tune that I recognized as "You've Got A Friend." She started to sing too, and it seemed like she was singing to me: "*Winter, Spring, Summer or Fall, all you got to do is call and I'll be there.*"

As she sang, I started to feel sad because I knew I could really only see her in the summer. She usually just played, but her voice sounded really good too.

When she finished, she looked at me and said, "My mother and stepfather are divorcing. My grandparents want us to stay with them, but I'll really miss my friends in Livonia."

I tried to be supportive, but I was thrilled at the idea that she might stay. "That would really be tough," I said using the empathic listening I'd read about in Dr. Stone's paper.

"But the good part is that I could stay with you. If I stay, do you want to be girlfriend-boyfriend at school?"

"Of course I want you as my girlfriend," I told her. "Will you want to hold hands and kiss in school?"

She started laughing. "Let's just do that outside of school. But I really do want to hold hands and kiss, okay?"

"That'll be great. We can meet here and have our private time."

"I'll get to see you play sports. I'm worried, though, that I won't know any of the girls. I hope they'll want to be my friends... Anyway, I've been working on another song. I want you to sing it. Ready?"

She played the opening notes to "Joy to World" by Three Dog Night, and I gladly sang it with a smile.

—✦—

The first day of high school came, and Teresa and I had agreed that we would play it cool and not have any public displays of affection. We'd also agreed that I would sit with Stan on the bus. Some girl sat with Teresa, but they didn't talk much.

I didn't see her much during the day at school, but after football practice met her at the docks to talk about the day.

Before we started talking, we hugged and kissed.

"I talked to several girls today," she told me. "It'll take time, but they were nice to me."

"Oh, good to hear."

"I told them I'd worked with you over the summer, and they seemed to like that. You're quite popular."

"I don't know about that. I just try to do well in my classes and sports."

"Tom, it seems like a lot of these girls want you as their boyfriend."

"Who?" I tried my best to keep a straight face, but I just burst out laughing.

"What's so funny?"

"Come on. It doesn't matter. I only want you."

"From what I could gather, Kate is considered the best-looking girl in the class, and the rumor is she likes you."

"Well, too bad. I like you." I didn't know if I should tell her the story about Kate or not, but then I said, "I was in French class with her in seventh grade, and she said she liked some guy named David. Anyway, I like you. Though now that you've had a look at all the studs at Walled Lake Central, I'll probably lose you."

She smiled really big and shook her head. "You won't."

We had our first football game against Milford. I had several tackles at defensive end. Both Bernie and Charlie had taught me some skills that really helped me, so even though I'd missed a season of defense, I felt really comfortable. I had practiced kicking and punting over the summer, so I got to handle the kickoff duties as well. Bernie had also really helped me with my kicking. The team really didn't get in a situation where we had to punt, but I was ready in case the coach decided we needed to kick it away on fourth down.

I started at quarterback and basically ran the blast running play or variations every time. I didn't throw any passes. Kenny, the new transfer student, played every other series, and when he was in, he passed the ball at least a third of the time. We both had success, and our team beat Milford 30-6.

Our next game was the following Wednesday against Farmington. I played pretty well, but we were down 13-6 at the half. However, the touchdown we'd scored had happened while I was at quarterback. I was also called on to try to kick the extra point, but the hold didn't get down in time, and my timing was off, so I missed it.

We continued to trail by a touchdown into the fourth quarter, and time was running out. Coach put Kenny in as quarterback, and he completed several passes and eventually found an open receiver over the middle to bring us within one point. For the extra point, we lined up in the triple-I formation. Kenny faked the blast play and ran around right end, and no one could catch him. He scored the two-point conversion, and we beat a tough Farmington team.

During the next week of practice, I continued as starting quarterback. I talked to Kenny, and he was such a nice guy about it. He seemed happy to be my backup. But I decided to talk to our coach after practice.

"Kenny's really playing well," I told Coach. "I'm not really adding a lot to the quarterback position. He runs better and can throw a whole lot better. The last two years, I was successful at quarterback because I could run over people, but the defenses are bigger and better, and I'm not running over people this year."

"Tom, you're our leader. The guys respond well to you and trust you. For some reason, when you're in at quarterback, the guys want to win for you."

"I appreciate that, Coach, but you and I both know I don't have the skills that Kenny does.

If you want to play him more at quarterback, I'd be happy to learn other offensive positions."

"We'll see. I might want to try you at the Y position, which is the first back through the hole on the blast play. Do you think you could knock a linebacker on his butt?"

"I bet I could."

"Let's try it, but for now, I need you as one of our quarterbacks."

I got to try out the Y position at the next practice, and I was okay, but I needed some work. I also got to try the position for just one series during the game against Farmington Harrison, but I didn't do great. Kenny probably got more snaps than me at quarterback because we trailed the entire game and needed passing to try to come back. We ended up losing.

On the way home, the whole team was talking on the bus, and Coach yelled back, "When I lost a game, I didn't say a word and cried all the way home."

We quickly stopped talking and didn't say anything. I looked over at Denny and saw tears in his eyes. I put my head down and didn't say another word.

I continued to practice the Y position, and it was obvious that Kenny was going to be our starter for the Waterford game. Some of the guys asked me about it, and Denny was really passionate about wanting me as the starting quarterback. I told him I supported Kenny and assured him that Kenny had a better arm and was faster than me.

— ✦ —

With the homecoming game and dance coming up, I asked Teresa to be my date. I then asked her if she could help me find girls who would want to go with Stan, Denny and Floyd.

"Shelley would love to go with Stan, but he'll have to call her," she told me. "Give him this number and tell him to call. And I think I know a couple girls who would go with Denny and Floyd. Give me until tomorrow.

The next day Teresa gave me a name and number for Floyd and a name and number for Denny. "These two girls are so nice," she told me. "They will say yes if the guys call them tonight."

"Melanie and Kay?" I asked.

"Do you know them?"

"Of course. They're both really nice. Thank you," I told her.

"Shelley called me," Teresa added with a big smile. "She said Stan called her. This will be so much fun."

Later that day I gave Floyd Melanie's number and Denny Kay's number. They were both really excited.

"This better not be a joke," Floyd said in his deep voice. "She said she'd go, right?"

Denny was more trusting. He just nodded and said thanks.

They each called that night, and the next day we all had dates for the homecoming dance.

When I saw Teresa that afternoon, she seemed a little distant. We agreed to meet that night at the docks.

"I wanted to tell you that I got a call last night and a guy asked me to the homecoming dance," she told me as soon as I got there.

"What?" I could hear my voice getting a little higher.

"This guy called and said he was new to the school district. His name's Kenny."

"Kenny called you."

"Yeah, he was so nice. I told him you were my boyfriend, and he said you were one of his best friends at school and on the football team but you'd never told him about me." She looked at me for a moment. "I know you don't want the PDA, but come on, Tom. What would it hurt to tell people we're going steady?"

"You're right. Everyone will know when they see us at the homecoming dance."

"I told Kenny to hurry up and call Kate. She doesn't have a date yet."

"Kate?"

"Yes, they'll make a great couple. I'm doing pretty well as a matchmaker, don't you think?"

I decided to come clean and tell her the whole story of Kate and me in the seventh grade. I figured she should hear it from me first, but I was too late. Kate had already told her the story from her perspective.

"She said she really liked you but was just too shy to talk to you," Teresa explained. "She said she was really hurt when you stopped walking with her. She was hoping you would date her this year since she's been working on not being so shy. I'm happy you told me the truth, Tom. I hope we have the type of relationship where we're honest."

"T, I've always been honest with you," I told her. "I just got nervous having to tell you about this."

Teresa leaned toward me, pressed her lips against mine and gave me a big smack.

The next week, the football team played Waterford, and we beat them soundly to go three and one for the season. Kenny started at quarterback, but I played three series at quarterback, and I kicked my first extra point. I also played well at defensive end.

Charlie, Bernie and Gramps all came out to the game, and I was glad they got to see a win.

On the bus ride home, the coach looked at all of us and said, "We won! Now we can celebrate."

We all started making a lot of noise and tried to remember some cheers.

Denny yelled out, "Ooo sah sah sah, ooo sah sah sah, hit 'em in the head with a big kielbasa!"

I created my own cheer based on my favorite food. "P-I-Z-Z-A, pizza, pizza pizza!" We all enjoyed the ride home.

"No I can't forget this evening,
Or your face as you were leaving.
But I guess that's just the way the story goes.
You always smile but in your eyes your sorrow shows,
Yes it shows."
— *Harry Nilsson (1971)*

Lucy Goosey

While Mark and I were separated, I started dating a guy my friend Katie introduced me to named Mike. I know his name sounds a lot like Mark, but he seemed like a good guy. Mike was from Chicago and took me to do a lot of fun things in the area. Yesterday he took me to a Cubs game. Mike was a Cubs fan, unlike Mark, and we had fun. During the seventh-inning stretch Harry Caray led the crowd in "Take Me Out to the Ballgame," and Mike and I sang along.

"You have such a raspy voice," I teased him. "Are you sure you never smoked?"

"I used to smoke."

"You did?" Before he'd told me he never smoked. "When did you quit?"

"Ah, recently."

"Recently? When?"

"Recently."

"Today?"

"Recently."

This really bothered me because he'd previously told me he wasn't a smoker. But I decided to wait until after the game to talk to him further about this.

When he took me home, I looked at him and said, "You deceived me into thinking you were never a smoker. And you didn't give me a straight answer about when you quit. Now that I think about it, your apartment and *you* smell like smoke. How did I miss this?"

"What's the difference? Why do you have to be so judgmental?" he asked. "Are you the anointed one?"

Since I'd read Dr. Stone's paper, I could see what was going on. I'd tried to bring up a difficult subject and get information. Mike hadn't shown understanding of my concerns and dismissed my questions, making no effort to answer them. "What's the difference" was certainly a dismissing statement. Then he used two blaming statements, trying to argue that he was right and I was wrong. Oh my. How am I going to find a boyfriend who treats girlfriends like it describes in Dr. Stone's paper?

"I don't want to argue," I told him. "Let's call it a night."

"Fine. You attack me and get all judgmental, and then you leave."

"I'm tired." I turned and started walking to my apartment.

As I went, I heard him yell, "Go sit on your throne, Queen Elizabeth. I hope you're happy."

I never looked back and never heard from him again.

The next day my phone rang.
"Lucy Davis?"
"Yes."

"This is Mrs. Young from the Human Resources department at the Detroit Free Press. We received your letter and resume, and we'd like to interview you. Would you be willing to interview for a feature editor position?"

"Yes. Thank you!"

"Are you available on either Friday, August twenty-fifth or Friday, September first?"

"Let me look at my calendar." I examined my date book and saw that September first was the Friday before Labor Day weekend. "Actually, September first would work out perfectly. I could spend Labor Day weekend with my parents in the Detroit area. Thank you so much."

"Great. I have you down to meet Mr. David Alton at one pm on September first. Do you know how to get to our building?"

"The building on West Lafayette Street?

"Yes."

"I'll be there. Thank you very much."

Once I hung up, I called my mom first and then my dad to tell them about my interview. This opportunity certainly softened the blow of Mike leaving.

After I talked to both my mother and father, I thought about calling Mark. It had been almost two months. But what would I say to him? Would I just tell him how excited I was about the opportunity? I decided to wait.

A few days later, the phone rang.

"Luce?"

"Hi, Mark. How've you been?"

"I first want to make sure it's okay that I called you. Today is August sixteenth. I know the summer isn't over, but we last saw each other on June sixteenth and it's now been two months."

"Mark! Oh my. You called after exactly two months. That's so sweet. Of course it's fine. How've you been?"

"I've been okay. The Sox have had a good year, but it is going to be hard to catch the A's. Luce, you're still my dream girl. I didn't like it, but I honored your two months. During this time, I've read the Dr. Stone paper several times. If you're still willing to date me, I hope you'll find I've learned a lot. I'd like to start with a clean slate."

"Oh, Mark, that's so sweet. I'd really like to go out with you. I've learned a lot too. I'm sure I'm far from perfect, but I would like to try the clean slate too. Two months ago, you asked me to Uno Pizzeria. I'd like to go there with you if you still want to go."

"All right. I could be over at six-thir...um, six-forty-five."

"Great, Mark. Um, hey, let's just make it anytime between six-thirty and seven. I'll be ready."

"Okay. See you soon!"

I was skeptical, but after this Mike situation and not meeting any other guys I liked better, I thought I should start being a little more flexible. What's the difference what time he gets here? I want to see him. I'll have to tell him about the interview.

I really do feel special right now. He didn't forget about me in the past two months, and he called on the day that was exactly two months. I'm really going to try to be a better girlfriend. If it doesn't work out this time, I want to say that I gave it my best.

At 6:44 Mark arrived, and he was carrying three roses.

"Aww, thank you."

"Luce, I've missed you. Here are two roses for the past two months and one for what I am hoping is a very good next month."

"Aww, you're so sweet."

"I want you to see that I'm trying. And if I start slipping up I'm willing to see Dr. Stone with you again."

"I don't know what to say. I'm overwhelmed. I missed you and almost called you, but I'm so happy it worked out this way."

"Are you hungry for some deep dish pizza?"

We had a good time that evening, and I really think we both appreciated each other so much more. I told Mark about my interview and asked him if he wanted to go with me and stay a couple days with my parents.

"Lucy, I don't want to lose you, and Dr. Stone's paper says couples should know each other's dreams and really support their partner in those dreams. I'd love to come with you, and I know you've always wanted to work for The Free Press. I fully support your dream, and I want you to get it. I also want to tell you that there was another commuter train crash a month ago. My dream is to get out of the train business."

The plan was for Mark to pick me up on Friday morning. I didn't want to be late for the interview, so I thought we should get to town and have some lunch first. Mark was at my house at seven thirty sharp. I had told him between seven thirty and eight. Who was this new guy?

"Good morning, sweetie," he said when he arrived. "I'm ready."

"Oh, Mark. Thanks for being here early. Are you all packed?" He nodded. "I still need another ten minutes, but I'll hurry."

Just a few minutes later, we headed off in Mark's Ford. I looked at him, just amazed that he was back in my life. "Why do you have on dress clothes?" I asked. "You don't have to come in with me, you know."

"Lucy, you're not going to believe this, but I got a call from a guy at Ford yesterday who wants me to come talk to him today," Mark said. "He seemed excited that I'd be in town today. He asked me to stop by and meet him after I dropped you off for the interview. My coat and tie are in the back. I didn't want to drive with them."

"What?" I was surprised. I'd talked to my dad about Mark's dream, and he'd promised to check in with Bernie about openings at Ford, but I never realized things might happen so fast.

"Your dad got my resume to Bernie, and he did a little detective work and found a guy hiring in Dearborn with my skills. I think the guy knows your brother too, because he mentioned both of them. Your family is so good to me!"

Wow. I was amazed, both at my family's kindness and that Mark had sent my dad his resume after I suggested it. "This is just unbelievable!" I told him. "Charlie and Bernie are very well liked and know a lot of people. Good luck!"

We had a very pleasant drive on I-94 East. This was so much different than our trip to Michigan over Memorial Day.

Mark dropped me off twenty minutes before the interview and I went in and waited. When it was my turn I first met with Mrs. Young, who had me fill out an application and salary requirements. My dad had told me ask for about a 15% increase in salary, so I had the number calculated and put it as my requirement, though I knew I'd probably be happy just to get my current salary.

She then took me to David Alton's office. He greeted me and asked me to sit down.

"So, Lucy Davis, you have great credentials. How can you help make The Detroit Free Press a better paper?"

I started right in, telling him it was my dream to work here. I told him I wouldn't shy away from the tough stories. I mentioned that I had a lot of experience and could help younger feature writers as well.

"Are there any features we aren't covering today that you believe would be a hit with our readers?"

I quickly thought and this is what came out: "I recently met with a psychologist who specializes in marriage counseling. She gave me a paper she wrote and told me that most people struggle with relationships. I read her paper and was fascinated by it. I'd love to do some writing about relationships. She actually works at Michigan State and has offices in the Detroit and Chicago areas. And I haven't presented this idea to the Sun Times yet."

Mr. Alton thought for a minute and said, "This sounds like a great idea. Could you save it for your work at The Free Press?" He put his hand out to shake mine. "I'm going to ask Mrs. Young to get an offer letter out to you. You're exactly what we need here at The Free Press. If the offer meets your expectations, would you be willing to work here?"

I hesitated for a minute. Should I tell him the New York Times is after me? "Mr. Alton, if you and the New York Times made me the same offer, I'd live my dream of working at The Free Press."

"Great. I hope to see you here soon. I'll have Mrs. Young get a moving package together for you too."

"Thank you so much."

It couldn't have gone any better. Now I just had to wait. I really hoped this all worked out.

I waited in the lobby for Mark to return. He finally got there about forty-five minutes after my interview had finished up.

"How'd it go, Luce?"

I nodded and smiled, but said, "I'll tell you all about it, but let's head to my dad's house. How'd it go at Ford?""

Mark got on the Lodge Freeway and said, "It couldn't have gone any better. I think they want to hire me! Harry, the guy I'd report to, is a friend of Charlie's and Bernie's. He's such a great guy. This would really be my dream to work in the same building as Henry Ford II. This's exactly what I want to do. But I just have to wait. They have one more person to interview."

"Wow, it sounds great. I hope you get it. My interview went great too. I really want this job."

"Luce, you know that clean slate idea? If we moved to Michigan, maybe we could really put Illinois behind us and treat each other well here."

I looked at Mark. He was saying all the right things. "I agree, and I really want that. I got asked a question, and I had to come up with something quickly. Mr. Alton asked me about something new I thought I could incorporate at The Free Press, so I told him about Dr. Stone's paper on healthy relationships."

"Did you tell him we were in counseling?"

"No." I laughed. "I just said I'd interviewed her. What's weird is that saying that might have sealed the deal."

We arrived at my dad's house, and after talking for a while and telling him and Ruth about the interviews, my dad asked Mark if he wanted to take a walk to the lake. Mark told me later that my dad had told him how proud he was of him for following through on the couple's counseling. He'd also said that if Mark ever wanted to marry me, and I wanted to marry him, he would welcome him with open arms.

I could tell this made Mark happy, but he and I agreed that we should see how these jobs worked out and how our clean-slate relationship went for some time before getting engaged.

Within two weeks I got an offer letter from The Free Press that met all my requirements. I gave my notice at The Sun Times and decided to live with my dad for two weeks and my mom for two weeks, giving me four weeks to explore the area before deciding where to move. Both of my parents had been good to me, and I wanted to spend time with each of them. My dad stored my furniture for me.

I'm sure I was the only editor from The Free Press living at home, and it felt a little weird to be back with my parents, but I told them it was just temporary until I figured out where I wanted to live.

On my last day with The Sun Times, Mark had still not heard from Ford. He called Harry, the man he'd interviewed with, to check on his status but was only able to leave a message with a clerical person.

It was sad for me to leave Mark, but on Saturday, September 30, I turned in the keys to my apartment, and a moving company took all my belongings to my dad's house. I drove by myself to my dad's, still hoping Mark would be moving to Michigan soon.

*"Did you ever read about a frog
who dreamed of being a king,
And then became one?
Well except for the names,
And a few other changes,
You can talk about me.
The story's the same one."*
— Neil Diamond (1971)

Homecoming

Bernie came over on Saturday. He said he'd
wanted to see me play football more than
he had, but it was hard for him to make it
out because the ninth grade team plays on
Wednesdays.

"Mom, do I still have a suit?" I asked as we
sat in the living room.

My mom smiled. "You do, but it won't fit
you. Have you measured your height recently?"

"I measure it all the time. I'm six-three now.
I'm one of the tallest kids in my class."

"You look six-three," Mom said. "That's why
all of your pants are too short already that we just
bought in August. And I have no idea how to buy a
suit."

"Let's all go. I'll help," said Bernie.

So we all headed out to the Pontiac Mall.

"We need to go to Hudson's," said Bernie
when we arrived.

"No, it's too expensive," my mom protested.

"Eve, sweetheart, I'm going to help. I know
these clothes are too expensive for you, but he

really can't go to a school dance with suit pants four inches too short."

We went to Hudson's. I'm glad Bernie was there because I was ready to get a bow tie and plaid pants. Instead he recommended a navy blue suit with a white shirt and a gold tie. I thought it really looked sharp. We kept shopping, and Bernie also helped me get a pair of blue jeans, a pair of khaki elephant bellbottom pants and a pair of brown bellbottom pants.

"These pants are a little long," I told them.

"Let's be safe. You might grow another inch in the next month."

When it came time to pay, Bernie footed the whole bill. "Eve, I'll pay for these clothes if you buy us a Little Caesar's pizza.

We picked up the 'za on the way home.

My mom agreed to drive us to the homecoming dance and back. First we picked up Shelley and Teresa. I thought I looked good, but *Wow!* Teresa and Shelley looked great. There was no doubt I'd have the best-looking date.

Next we stopped by Stan's house. His mother came out and asked us all to come in. She had a new camera and wanted to take pictures. I could tell Stan was a little embarrassed when his mother asked him to go stand with Shelley.

"Put your arm around her," she instructed.

Watching Stan made the picture-taking a fun time. We then got back in my mother's Chevy and headed to the dance.

We walked in, and reality hit. We were all freshmen. Almost everyone was older than us. We quickly looked for the other freshmen. We found Denny, Floyd and Kenny and went to join them.

"Men," I said, lowering my voice a little and nodding my head. This got a smile out of the guys. "How'd you get these great-looking ladies to go out with you?"

Denny said, "We're all wondering the same thing about you."

"Does everyone know everyone?" I asked, trying to use my manners.

"No, who's Stan's date?" said Floyd in his naturally low voice.

I looked at Stan and could tell he would be more comfortable if I introduced her, so I said, "This is Stan the Man's date, Shelley. She goes to Livonia Bentley where Teresa would have gone if she hadn't moved here. You guys dance yet?"

"No, we're waiting for The Machine to lead the way," said Denny.

I started moving my shoulders up and down. "Hey, we're a team. We have to go out together, and we'll have to ask these gorgeous ladies to grace us with their presence."

"Tom, please. Let's just dance." Teresa grabbed my hand and dragged me out onto the dance floor.

Denny, Kay, Floyd and Melanie followed us out, but Kenny, Kate, Stan and Shelley stayed back. Those of us on the dance floor got into it pretty quickly. It was good to start off with a fast dance so all we had to do was shake and not try to dance with our dates. Dancing was a way to act silly and get away with it.

When we came off the dance floor, we ran into a couple other guys from the freshman football team. Both were decked out in classic disco outfits and didn't bring dates. One guy had his curly hair in about a six-inch afro. We talked to them for a while.

"We thought we'd come check this out to see if there were any single chicks," the other explained.

"Found any?" Floyd asked.

"Oh yeah, and since they don't have dates, they all want to dance. Watch this."

The two guys walked up to a couple girls and took them out on the dance floor. If I thought we'd been moving around on the dance floor, these guys were really moving. They were quite entertaining. I never knew offensive lineman could move so well.

I was relieved to see that there were no silly kissing booths like at the junior high dances. People actually danced at the high school events.

At one point a little later in the evening, they announced the homecoming queen and her attendants. I was most interested in knowing who won the freshman attendant. Kay and Kate were two of the five in the running. Unfortunately, Teresa didn't get nominated. I guess she was too new and people didn't know her. Of course she told me that if I'd been a little more public with our dating, more people would know her by now.

All of the nominees and their dates came to the front of the dance floor. So because Denny and Kenny were the dates of nominees, they went as well. There was a little suspense and then Kate was announced as our freshman attendant. They took pictures of her and Kenny.

When they came back over, we all congratulated her. Kenny and Kate really seemed to hit it off, and I could tell Teresa took a little pride in knowing it was because of her that they'd come together.

I smiled at Kenny. "Man, first you take my position on the football team and now you're on the homecoming court."

"I play basketball and baseball too, so look out," he told me.

We all laughed.

Near the end of the evening, the DJ announced that if you had a very special lady in your life, now was the time to bring her to the dance floor. So we all brought our dates and stood in the center of the room.

"Now, everyone get really close for this last slow song," said the DJ.

None of us really seemed to know how to slow dance, so we all just put our arms around our dates' waists and swayed back and forth. I looked at Stan, and he was kissing Shelley, that sly devil. He acts so shy most of the time.

Teresa saw this too and smiled. "Tom, it has been so wonderful to be here with you. I'm with the tallest, best-looking, most athletic and sweetest guy in the class."

I looked at her and knew I had to respond with something. "It's my pleasure to be here with the most beautiful and talented girl in the class. I wouldn't want to be with anyone else."

She looked at me and leaned in for a kiss, but I hesitated and looked around.

"I don't ask for too much PDA, but it would mean a lot if you would kiss me during this dance," she said.

So I put my lips on hers and felt that helpless yet excited feeling all over again. I would follow her anywhere.

— ✦ —

With the homecoming dance over, we were back at football practice the following Monday. We were doing well in football with a record of 6-1. Floyd, Stan and I were really playing well on defense, and the offense seemed to be a little more potent now that Kenny was getting into the flow and making good passes to the receivers. I had actually caught three passes in the past three games from the Y position, which I played more and more. I was also getting better at knocking the linebacker down. Many times when Denny and I played the blast backs together, we would each knock the linebackers down and let our running backs go for big yardage.

For our second-to-last game of the season, we had to travel to West Bloomfield. We all knew they would be good. However, we had the confidence that we could beat them. But confidence or no confidence, we were down 21-0 at the half. Anything that could go wrong seemed to have gone wrong. For example, when I lined up in punt formation, the snap sailed ten feet over my head, and I ended up losing twenty yards on the play.

I mainly just played quarterback now when we were up big and just running the ball. Kenny was our quarterback for the second half, and he came out trying to pass. The problem was the receivers weren't open, and he was getting a lot of pressure from the West Bloomfield pass rushers, so he was getting very frustrated.

We got in the huddle and instead of calling the play, he yelled at his teammates, "Come on line, *block*!"

I grabbed a hold of his facemask and gave him a very stern look. "Everyone's trying their best to do their job," I said. "Now you do your job!" I pushed him out of the huddle.

After a moment he came back and called the play and never said a word to the others the rest of the game. I did have a presence about me, as I was six to eight inches taller than most of the others.

We lost the game 35-0, and afterward Kenny apologized.

"Kenny, it's okay," I told him. "It was a very frustrating game for all of us. You've got the talent to be a great quarterback, but you don't have the rapport with the team to say something negative like that. With offensive linemen, you really have to be their friend and gain their respect. I have that relationship with them, but I can't throw the ball like you. They needed me to step in and defend them. I'm sorry I pushed you."

After that, Kenny and I became closer friends. I knew he was grateful that I'd recommended him for starting quarterback.

We still had one game left to play—against our crosstown rival, Walled Lake Western. Beating Western could save our season. Finishing 7-2 sounded a lot better than finishing 6-3. I knew a bunch of the guys on the opposing team from playing on the Red Devils years ago.

I could tell our Coach really wanted to win the game. He had a pep talk with us before the game like no other. His voice went from quiet to very loud as he attempted to pump us up:

"Okay, men, this is Western. You need to BLOW 'EM OFF THE FIELD! This is the difference between good and great." He held his thumb and forefinger an inch apart. "Give me that much more today! You can hit somebody or you can HIT SOMEBODY. NOW GET OUT THERE AND DO IT!"

He kicked over a chair as we all got up and headed out. We felt the fire, and I know I gave more than I normally would've given.

Several of our players (including me) liked our long hair down to our shoulders, but there were at least five guys on the Western team who had ponytails out of their helmets and halfway down their backs.

We wanted to win, but they were a tough team. I had kicked six extra points throughout the season but still had never kicked a field goal.

In the fourth quarter, with the game tied 21-21, we got the ball down to the four yard-line but then got a holding penalty. It was fourth down with nineteen yards to go when Coach called for the field goal. He looked at me and said, "Tom, we need this."

I ran to the huddle and told everyone what the coach had said. I looked at all of them. We needed this to go well. The team lined up, and the snap was good. Kenny did a good job holding the ball, and I kicked it through. It wasn't the prettiest field goal, but it got over the crossbar.

Then there were still three minutes left to play, and we had to kick off to Western. The coach kept yelling, "DEFENSE! DEFENSE!

Western picked up a first down. On the next play, the quarterback went back to pass, but Floyd, Denny and I were all coming directly at him. He threw a wild, off-balance pass, and any of us could have intercepted it, but Floyd caught it and ran the other way for a touchdown with Denny and me right beside him as his escorts. We won the game 31-21 and celebrated like crazy.

I was especially excited because Bernie had made it out to his second game. I think he took the day off work to make sure he made it. And Charlie was there too. It was great to see them after the game.

However, the celebration didn't last too long because basketball practice started the very next day. Only twelve kids came out for the basketball team. Six of us had played football, so it was a rough transition. I'd never felt so out of shape in my life. I guess football shape and basketball shape are totally different. I huffed and puffed running the drills.

It was great that Kenny and Stan were on the team, but the starting lineup had been the same for the past two years of junior high school. Paul Barnes was now 5'7" and the point guard. Chad McCoy was 5'8" and played the other guard. The forwards and center were all close to 6'0". Kent Herring, like Paul and Chad, did not play football and they'd practiced basketball all fall. However, the two forwards, Larry Kemp and Steve Thompson from my seventh grade history class, both played football too.

I was now 6'4". There was another guy named Rob Jalkanen on the team who was 6'5", but he hadn't played a lot of basketball. This guy talked very differently from everyone else, and I soon learned he was a yooper, which is what people from the upper peninsula of Michigan are called. For the word *yes*, he would say *ya*. He also ended most sentences with *eh* and a voice inflection like he was asking us if we understood.

The other three guys from the football team were my buddy Stan Franciszek, who was now 5'10", Mark Nelson, who was now 6'1", and Kenny Gibson, my fellow quarterback in football was 5'9". Both Stan and Mark had played in junior high, and Kenny had started on his 8th grade team. So of course, we all wanted to play as much as we could.

The other two guys on team, I didn't know well. Jim Whitman was 5'9" and was known more for tennis. Tom Brown was 6'1", and I had only heard of him as a golfer. I wasn't used to playing on the same team as another Tom, but I'm not sure Coach JR Reese, who was also a gym teacher, actually knew his first name, so it didn't matter much. He always called him Brown.

.

"Doctor, my eyes have seen the years,
And the slow parade of fears without crying,
Now I want to understand.
I have done all that I could
To see the evil and the good without hiding,
Now you must help me if can."
— *Jackson Browne (1972)*

Roger That

When Louise and Stan got back from their trip to Indiana, I tried to be nice to her, but she was very distant. There was no warm greeting. All she could say was that the house was mess. And Stan couldn't wait to get over to the docks to talk to Tom.

After he left, I asked Louise how her trip went.

"I had a great time. I think I've finally realized that I can be happy after we divorce," she said.

"Divorce? Louise, I missed you."

"Please. Don't give me that. I've been in this marriage way too long to fall for anything like that."

I wasn't expecting a serviceman's welcome, but she was colder than I'd ever imagined. Maybe it *was* over.

Grasping at straws, I said, "I'll contact Dr. Stone and see when we can come in."

"We're done with Dr. Stone," she told me. "Were you able to look for somewhere to live while I was gone?"

I could tell I wasn't going to get anywhere with her. "No, I'll contact a realtor in the morning," I said.

We hardly spoke the rest of the night. Louise was on the phone most of time catching up with friends and family.

The next morning, I kissed her on the check when I got out of bed. I could see her smile a little, but she never opened her eyes. I left her a note that I was going to the Century 21 office.

When I arrived, I was greeted by a very attractive lady. Looking at her, I almost forgot why I'd come.

"Hi, I'm looking for a house."

"Are you looking to sell your current house?"

"No. My wife wants to divorce me, so I need to find another place."

"I'm surprised anyone would want to divorce a good-looking man like you."

Was this my lucky day? I go hunting for a house and find a great lady who appreciates me?

She offered to show me some possible homes that weren't too far away, so I rode in her car with her. She said she'd have to call to get appointments for the showings, but she was very nice to me, so I figured she liked me and wanted to go out.

"Which house do you like the best, you handsome devil?" she said.

"I think we should go to dinner and figure out which one is the best," I suggested.

All of a sudden her mood changed. "I'm sorry. I need to get home to my husband and children, but call me and let me know what you decide," she said quickly.

How did I misread that one? When I was a young professional baseball player I couldn't miss with the ladies. Now I'm a middle-aged factory worker.

I went home, and Louise asked me how it went.

"Terrible. I don't want to leave you. I don't want to go live in another house. I want to watch Stan play sports. I'm sorry I've been such a bad husband, but I want the rest of this year as a final test to make sure we really want to get a divorce."

Louise looked at me. "Rog, if we give this one more try, I really want some effort. I don't want a half-hearted effort where you're spending your time looking up and down at every lady you see. And do you promise me that if I still want a divorce by the end of the year, you'll leave?

"Weeze, I agree."

I reached over and gave her a hug. "Would you like to go to the Little Brown Jug in Union Lake and get some pizza?"

"Sure."

I just don't know what it is. Louise is very pretty, and I'm proud to have her as my wife. I just can't understand why I have to try to hunt down every pretty lady I see. I decided I should talk this over with Dr. Stone, whether Louise wanted to go anymore or not.

At the Little Brown Jug, we laughed and had a good dinner. When we got back, I sat next to her with my arm around her as we watched TV.

Before we went to bed I said, "Would you mind if I tried to schedule with Dr. Stone? I want to make sure I'm really on track to try to be the best husband for you."

Louise said she had no problem with me meeting with Dr. Stone, and I was able to call the next day and get an appointment with her after work.

After giving her an update on the past few weeks, I said, "I don't understand why I can't keep my eyes on my own wife. I realize I've created the damage in this relationship. How can I move forward and only think about my wife?"

"It's not unusual for men to notice good-looking ladies," Dr. Stone said. "But most men have developed a thinking strategy that keeps them from getting in trouble. When they see a lady who appeals to them, they acknowledge that she's good-looking, but they immediately say to themselves: my wife is not only good-looking but she loves me, she supports me, she's honest, she's reliable, she's a good mother, she's a great cook, and above all she puts up with me every day, and I love her. I want to be with my wife forever. I don't know what the problems are with this other lady, but there are some."

"Try to think long term," she continued. "Men get married because they want to be with a lady for the long run. Some men think short term and want to get any lady with legs in bed. Sure, they might get that, but they'll face problems when they don't call her the next day. Do you want to try this thinking strategy?"

"I really do."

"Right now you have an out. You can go get a place of your own. You can still attend all of Stan's games, and you can date whoever you want. Doesn't that sound exciting?"

"I've thought that way for a lot of years," I told her. "I neglected my wife, yet she stood by me.

I think what happened is that I wasn't planning on getting married. I didn't decide Louise was the lady for me, that I wanted to be with her forever. She got pregnant. I wanted a child, and she seemed good enough."

"You sacrificed your years of dating to be with the lady who was giving birth to your child."

"I did, and we've had a marriage that was not all that romantic. We've had a marriage of living together, and I was able to coach my son in baseball and basketball. With just a little more effort, she would have been fine with me as her husband. But I've just had such a hard time turning off the prowl."

"You didn't turn off the prowl, but Louise still loved you."

"Now I have to turn off the prowl or she'll leave me. I'm ready to try it, but I might need your help."

"Roger, let's do this," said Dr. Stone. "You're trying to break a habit, and habits are not easily broken. Would you come see me each week for the next three weeks? After these sessions, if we think we've been able to work out a thinking strategy to break this habit, let's start couples therapy again. Would you go home and explain this to Louise?"

"Explain this to Louise? She'll be furious!"

"I really think you need to be honest with her and let her know what we're working on. Remember, when communicating with her, use a soft startup and throw her a good pass. Don't just go home and say, 'I'm working on not lusting after every woman with legs.'"

I laughed. "Thanks, Dr. Stone. I'll try it."

When I got home, I didn't see Louise, so I looked for her. When I found her, I wrapped my arms around her and said it was good to see her.

"How'd it go?"

"Maybe we should sit down if we're going to talk," I suggested.

She agreed, and we went out and sat on the couch.

"I went to the appointment today because my goal is to learn how to be a better husband for you. I haven't been the best husband."

She had the chance to rub it in a little and say something like *that's for sure*, but she didn't. She said, "I appreciate you going to the appointment.

"I have the most gorgeous, wonderful lady right here in my home, but yet I look too much at other women." I tried to soften it a little. *Lust* would have been too strong for her. I hoped I'd thrown a good pass.

"Can she help you?"

"I believe so. I fell into some short-term-thinking problems when I should have been focusing more long term. I have lost sight of the fact that the love of my life lives with me. I'm sorry. Dr. Stone believes she can help me if I attend sessions for the next three weeks. If I can show improvement and you're still willing, we can try couples therapy again after that."

"I know where your short-term brain is located," Louise said, her eyebrows raised.

I smiled. "You're right. And I only want to use that one with you."

She shook her head and smiled. "I said I'd support you. Let's see how it goes."

So I went back to therapy the next week.

"I'm really trying to use the thinking strategies, but I still notice ladies," I told Dr. Stone. "Is something wrong with me?"

"Unfortunately, all mammals are designed to hunt for mates. If you were a rabbit, there would be nothing wrong with you. However, in American culture for human beings, we're supposed to use our big frontal cortex and delay gratification for good executive decisions."

"So I think like an animal. I think I'm more of a wolf than a rabbit. And my wife says I think with my little brain."

Dr. Stone smiled. "You do think with the little ancient brain that all animals have called the limbic system, but it's buried deep behind your frontal cortex and not located in any other part of the body. By really thinking, you're forcing yourself to use the frontal cortex. By repeating the good things about your wife, you're delaying gratification and not trying to fondle every female you see."

"This makes sense. I'll keep working on it."

"What have you been doing for positive interaction with Louise?"

"That's going well. I kiss her on the cheek when I leave. I greet her when I get home. I ask her about her day. I sit with her to watch television. I've also been taking her to the Little Brown Jug every week for pizza and an adult beverage."

"Is she responding well?"

"Not as well as I would like. It seems she's just waiting for me to fail so she can say I told you so."

"She's hurt. She's probably still punishing you for hurting her. You need to step it up a little."

"What else can I do?"

"You need to do something to make her feel like she's really the special lady in your life."

I pondered this.

Dr. Stone said, "Why don't you stop at the grocery store and buy her something you wouldn't normally buy her?"

"The grocery store? Like the A&P? What would I get? A watermelon?"

"Stop at the grocery store, look around and decide what you could buy to make her feel special."

"All right."

"See you next week," Dr. Stone said as I left.

On my way home, I stopped at the A&P and looked around. What could I buy Louise to make her feel special? I finally came upon some steaks. I could grill these for her. Maybe I should get some corn-on-the-cob too. I kept walking through the store and decided to also pick up some vanilla ice cream and Hersey's syrup. As I got ready to check out, I saw some roses. This might be too much. Oh well. I picked up two roses to signify my second week of individual therapy.

When I got home I greeted Louise and told her I'd stopped to pick up food on the way home.

"Oh, Roger, you're so sweet. Roses?"

Dr. Stone was right. Louise liked the roses and the food. We enjoyed cooking the steaks, and she seemed to change her attitude toward me after that night. We started sitting together at Stan's games and seemed like a couple again.

After I'd completed two more weeks of individual therapy, we had a couples session. The only negative thing Louise brought up was that I still looked at ladies.

Dr. Stone helped out a lot and told her all men look at ladies, but she needed to trust that I had developed thinking strategies so I wouldn't want any other lady but her.

I had changed my thinking, but it was still going to take time for Louise to change her thinking habits. Dr. Stone cautioned that I had done my part, but I still had the option of leaving in January if Louise didn't respond well

.

"What they do?
They smile in your face.
All the time they want to take your place.
The back stabbers."
— O'Jays (1972)

Difficult Transition

Teresa and I were getting along great. She liked all of my friends, and she had become best friends with Kate, of all people. Kate was popular—especially now that she was the new homecoming attendant for our class—but Teresa liked her because she was really down to earth and quiet. I got to know Kate too. She seemed a lot different than when I'd tried to talk to her our seventh-grade year.

I continued to meet Teresa at the docks even though it was getting a little colder. We just wore more and more clothes. It was going on six months with her, and the magic was still there. There was no other girl I would want over her. Even if Susan Dey, my favorite actress from *The Partridge Family*, wanted me, I would keep Teresa. My goal was to keep this relationship going.

Given classes and sports, there wasn't a lot of time for each other, but we made time. I did something with Teresa every weekend. Sometimes we would just go over to each other's houses and listen to music. Often we would play guitar and sing. Music was our common bond.

Bernie and I were also really getting along great. He took time to listen to me and talk sports.

He seemed to enjoy my mother's company as well. My mother seemed happy most of the time, but sometimes she seemed frustrated when he didn't come to visit.

One day at basketball practice, I saw our coach talking to the varsity coach. I didn't know what they were talking about, but they were looking at me. I kept shooting baskets and warming up until the varsity coach walked up and told me how much he valued me and how he wanted me on the varsity team in a couple years— maybe even next year if I worked hard. I never started a game in middle school, but at 6'4" he saw me as a potential varsity basketball player now.

After running several drills, the freshman coach, Coach Reese, told us we would be scrimmaging. We all wore these reversible T-shirts so we could scrimmage, with one team wearing navy blue and the other team wearing yellow.

He called out the names to get us organized: "Phil Barnes, Chad McCoy, Steve Thompson, Larry Kemp, and Tom Mochina, wear yellow. Everyone else wear blue."

So that's what the coaches were talking about. I was going to work out with the starting unit. As Gramps had told me, if given an opportunity, make the most of it. So I was determined to play well.

The other four starters and Kent Herring got in a quick huddle. I could tell they weren't too pleased that I was playing with them. Barnes did most of the talking. I just listened and tried to make the most of my opportunity like anyone would. I knew if I didn't play well I would be back on the second team. Kent was a year older because he'd been held back, and he was once the tallest boy in the class but not anymore.

"Yellow team, play zone defense. Mochina in the middle with Kemp and Thompson down low and McCoy and Barnes up top. Now, let's have Franciszek, Gibson, Herring, Nelson and Jalkanen play offense."

Mark Nelson had played offensive and defensive tackles on the football team. He had played with me on the Red Devils two years ago and had a hard time making weight back then.

We all lined up in our positions.

"Get your arms up, Mochina," said Barnes.

I looked around and several of the other guys hadn't put their arms up yet, so I waited until Coach Reese gave the offense the ball. Why did Barnes yell at me and not the others? Why did he say anything at all when it wasn't time to put our arms up? I just ignored him.

When the play started, we all put our arms up, and we moved based on where the ball was.

"Mochina, move down!" yelled Barnes.

I looked at the position I was in and then looked at Coach Reese, and it seemed I was in the proper position.

"Mochina, move up!" yelled Barnes.

I moved up, and a defender slid behind me and scored.

"Mochina! Why'd you move up and let the player behind you?" yelled Coach Reese.

"Maybe if Barnes would keep his mouth shut, we'd play better defense? He yelled to me to move up."

"Since when do you listen to Barnes? Listen to me."

A few plays later, Barnes yelled at me again. When the play stopped, I walked up to him and yelled right in his face, "Do you have a problem?" I gave him about the meanest look I could.

"Barnes, Mochina, both of you run laps. Let's get a couple other people in who can play D. Whitman and Brown, get in there," said Coach Reese.

We started to run, but I was still talking to Barnes. "What's your problem? Are you trying to lose?"

"It's only practice. You don't know what you're doing. Kent's been working hard and needs to be in there if we want to win. The coaches will get it right."

"You say that, but you have no idea how hard I've worked."

"I've seen you play. You might be some hot-shot football player, but you're a backup on the basketball team."

"We'll see. Maybe you'll be the backup."

Barnes shook his head and laughed.

"Mochina, Barnes, get back in there. I want to see some defense from you, and if either of you talk, just start running."

On the next play, Kenny gave a head fake and Barnes got caught in the air. He shot and made the basket. I didn't have time to get there and contest the shot.

"Coach, I need Mochina to get here faster if the guy gets by. We didn't have this problem last year," said Barnes.

"We need you to keep your feet and not get faked out of your jock," Coach countered. "You spend too much time thinking about other people and too little time playing defense. Go run two laps and sit out. Gibson, I want to see you on D and Whitman back on offense. But first, you guys look gassed. Everyone take a blow."

Everyone ran to the drinking fountains and I followed until I heard, "Mochina!"

I turned around and walked back to coach. "You look good on defense, but no jobs are guaranteed. You really need to keep working."

"I will, Coach."

"Some of these guys who only play basketball don't want football players getting their playing time. If we're going to win this year, we're going to have to learn to exist together. I'll deal with Barnes and the others. Don't get into it with him. That's what he wants. It looks like I've got some deep talent, so a lot of guys might play."

"I understand. Thanks, Coach."

I've learned the less you say to the coach, the better. He only wants to know a player understands.

After the break, we continued practice with Barnes sitting out much of the scrimmage.

—◆—

On Saturday, Kenny, Stan, Denny and I all went over to Floyd's house. Floyd's dad had a reel-to-reel video system.

"Hey, men! I want to show you this."

Floyd turned on a clip of The Temptations performing "My Girl." We all watched. I couldn't help myself but to chime in on "*I got so much honey the bees envy me.*"

When the song ended, Floyd said, "We got this!"

"We got what?" said Kenny.

Floyd smiled and then said in his very low voice, "The talent show. We got this. You guys hip? Now, normally the best singer should play Ruffin, but we need a high voice for the part, so The Machine, you're the lead?"

"So we're going to sing and dance this?" I asked.

"The only way we'll win is if we do both. We'll have the tape of the song playing softly and we'll sing over it. Let's practice."

I'm not sure how good we were, but we had a lot laughs and a good time.

"Next Saturday you guys come back and we'll practice again."

"I got an idea," said Kenny. Let's get our homecoming dates to come onstage, and we'll sing to them."

"I like it," said Stan, "but my date was from another school."

"Stan, this is called acting. We'll just have another girl sit in. No big deal," responded Floyd.

"Make sure she's hot," said Stan, and we all started laughing.

When the talent show was first announced, Teresa and I had talked about us singing while she played guitar for "I Got You, Babe." We'd sung it many times on the picnic table at the docks, but she didn't want to do it as freshmen. However, she did agree to sit in a chair onstage while we did our version of "My Girl."

The next Thursday was Thanksgiving. The tradition the past three years had been for me to go with Gramps and his family to the parade. This year, my mom, Bernie and Bernie's two children all came too. Teresa and her mom came, and we all met up with Gramps, his three children and all his grandchildren.

While we were waiting for the parade, Mark, Lucy's boyfriend, got up and started speaking to all of us. "This year I learned a valuable lesson. I learned that if you don't really work on your relationship, you might lose it. I almost lost mine. I didn't work on my relationship with Lucy. Lucy's dad asked us to try couple's counseling, and I did poorly at that and lost Lucy for the summer. But I kept reading this paper about relationships and waited for my chance to once again date my dream girl. I wasn't sure I was going to get the chance. Anything could have happened. Lucy, would you please come over by me?"

I looked at Teresa, and she looked at me. I looked at my mom and I saw a tear in her eye. Everyone waited with anticipation.

When Lucy approached, Mark got down on one knee and took her hand. "My dear Lucy, I love you with all my heart. Even when we were apart, I never stopped loving you. But even with all my love, I still wasn't a good enough boyfriend for you. I hope you've seen in the past three months that I still have the same love, but I've learned essential communication skills that'll help us in the future."

Almost everyone gasped and there were more tears.

"I asked Santa Claus to bring you a special gift and give it to you at the end of the parade, but he's too busy with the key to the city. So he asked me to give you this." Mark pulled out a small box and gave it to Lucy. "My dear Lucy, I'd like you to be my wife."

By now Lucy was crying, and she grabbed Mark and hugged him. They hugged for a couple minutes, and then Mark looked at her and said, "I got the job with Ford. I start on Monday. I wanted it to be a surprise. But now, most importantly, I need your answer.

"Yes, yes, yes!" said Lucy and everyone started to congratulate them.

That was so sweet. I hope I can say even half of that when I ask Teresa to marry me someday. I looked at Teresa's mother. She was probably crying the most because she just went through a divorce. I then looked at Bernie. He looked shell-shocked. I wondered if someday he would ask my mother to marry him.

We again enjoyed the parade, and I couldn't help but look at Gramps to watch him check out Christmas Carol. I heard Gramps tell Mark he looked forward to seeing his future grandchildren at the parade someday.

After the parade, Teresa went to have Thanksgiving at her house, which was the home of her grandparents, and Mom and I went to visit Grandpa and Grandma Mochina, my mother's parents. This year, Bernie and his kids came too. Everyone there called Bernie Guy, and I did too at first so I didn't confuse everyone. I enjoyed visiting with my cousin Rod who was home from the service. It was weird seeing him with really short hair.

We continued the tradition of telling what we were thankful for. When it came to me, I said, "I know I've always been tall for a boy, but I am really thankful that I grew to six foot four. I'm very thankful for all of my friends. They crack me up. I have one very special friend, Teresa, and I am very thankful that she's come back into my life. I'm thankful for all of my family members, and Rod, I'm so thankful that you haven't gone off to war. I'm thankful for my mom. Without her, none of my activities would be possible. She's my biggest supporter. Lastly, I'm very thankful for getting to spend time with Guy, who I call Bernie. Bernie, it's been a special year having you in my life. Last but not least, I'm thankful for Carl and Karen. You guys make me smile."

> "Everybody plays the fool sometime,
> There's no exception to the rule.
> Listen Baby, it may be factual, may be cruel.
> I ain't lyin'. Everybody plays the fool."
> — *The Main Ingredient (1972)*

Throwing Bad Passes

On Monday after Thanksgiving, we had basketball practice. We now had only two more practices before our game on Wednesday. We went through all our drills, and I thought I was doing fairly well.

"Okay, men, let's scrimmage," said Coach. "This will be the first unit for the game on Wednesday. If you guys still don't like each other, you better figure it out really quickly because I've got twelve guys I feel comfortable playing and will sub you in a minute if you're not playing well. Man, even these skinny kids, Whitman and Brown, are really getting after it defensively."

"Center will be Mochina. Forwards are Thompson and Nelson. Guards will be Gibson and Barnes," said Coach Reese. I was pleasantly surprised to see Mark and Kenny starting. Coach had decided to start four football players with Barnes.

"Everyone else, blue jerseys. Let's start with Whitman and Franciszek at guards. McCoy, I'll switch you in. Herring and Kemp at forwards. Brown, you start at center, and I'll switch you off with Jalkanen.

I had been hoping Jalkanen would be my opposing center, because he plays much softer than Brown. Brown fouls a lot. If he does get any playing time, he'll probably foul out quickly.

On the first play, Kenny got a steal and headed down the outside. He passed it to Barnes in the middle who flipped the ball over his back, but I was too close to the hoop and the ball headed back down the court. Brown picked it up for two points.

"What are you guys doing?" Coach asked. "That was terrible."

"If Mochina knew the plays, he would have been right behind me and would have gotten the pass and scored."

"Mochina, did you say trailer?"

"No, Coach."

"Barnes did you hear Mochina say trailer?"

"I sure did, but he wasn't there."

The coach rolled his eyes and yelled, "I don't need this! It's not like we've got the best talent in the conference. We have to play well to win."

The next time down, Barnes passed me the ball, but he threw it at my feet. I was able to pick it up, turn and score off the backboard, but I thought Barnes passed the ball poorly on purpose. I could see Kenny getting frustrated because Barnes was bringing the ball up the court almost every time. Mark was getting frustrated too because he wasn't getting the ball.

A little later in the scrimmage, I got the pick from Mark and was wide open on the right block. Barnes threw a terrible bounce pass that hit the ground four feet from where I was. This time I'd had enough and didn't care if I started or not if Barnes was going to be on the floor.

I yelled, "Barnes, what's wrong with you? Don't you know how to throw a good pass, or do you only throw good passes to certain people?"

He looked away and said, "Shut up, Mochina."

I ran toward him and grabbed his shirt and yelled in his face. "Look, you may be a loser, but everyone else out here wants to win." Since I had a hold of his shirt, I shook him a few times before Coach Reese came over.

"Tom, Paul, you guys go sit out the rest of practice." This was the first time he'd called any of us by our first names.

"Coach, why am I sitting out? Don't you see what's going on? Barnes is messing up every play."

"Your job is to play the best basketball you can. Not all of your teammates can throw good passes."

I looked at him, and I knew I'd better sit down because I was hot. How come everyone can't get along like on the football team?

After a little more of the scrimmage, Coach announced, "Everybody except for Mochina and Barnes, hit the showers. I've got to figure out a new lineup. Every time I try to find a first team, they get beat by the second team."

He walked over to us. "Do you guys want to play basketball, because I know the wrestling team has some vacant weight classes?

"Coach, Mochina can't catch a good, hard pass. He just hasn't played enough basketball."

"Don't give me that. Do you think I'm blind? My seventy-seven-year-old mother can throw better passes than you," Coach said. "Here's the deal, I've got ten other guys who've worked hard and want to play. If I see any purposely thrown bad passes, any ball hogging or any yelling at another player, you won't play in the game on Wednesday. As of right now, you're both on the second team. Now, get your showers and come back tomorrow with good attitudes.

The next day the coach announced the new starting lineup, which was the same except Brown was playing center and Stan was playing the other guard. Barnes was on his best behavior, and so was I. The practice went well with everyone seeking playing time.

Our first game was a non-conference game against Detroit Pershing, an all-black school that was a powerhouse every year. In the '70s in metropolitan Detroit, the high schools were either almost all white or almost all black. There wasn't a lot of racial integration. We used the same starting lineup we'd used at practice, but only a few minutes into the game, the Doughboys were already up 10-0, and Brown had three fouls. Coach called timeout.

He put me in for Brown at center. "The tallest Pershing player is about six feet. If we run the baseline screen for Mochina, they won't be able to defend it, but guards, you have to take care of the ball," he explained.

On our first possession, Mark, who was a big, solid player, set a screen on my player on the left block, and I ran to the right block. Kenny threw me the ball right above my head, and I was able to catch it, turn and put it off the board and in before the defender fought through the pick. This play ended up working three more times, once each from Kenny, Stan and Whitman, before the Pershing coach had to change to a zone. Three different guards could throw me a good pass, so I knew Barnes could if he wanted to.

Barnes and McCoy came in for the guards with two minutes left in the first quarter. They came in with the mindset that they were going to drive through the Pershing zone and score, and it didn't work.

To start the second quarter, Jalkanen came in for me at center but only for about three minutes until Pershing went back to a zone defense. Coach Reese put Mark, Steve and me back in to play with Barnes and McCoy at guards.

It didn't go well. Barnes kept trying to do everything himself. Finally, he saw me cut to the right block and bounced the ball at my feet, which I wasn't able to handle. Coach Reese immediately called timeout and put Kenny in for Barnes.

"We've got to get someone in the game who can catch," said Barnes.

Coach Reese looked at him a minute and then said, "Barnes, your spot is at the very end of the bench so I don't have to see your face or hear from you for the entire game. Now get down there and get out of my huddle."

We trailed 35-16 at the half and went on to lose 68-31. I started the second half, and Barnes didn't play at all. I ended up with 15 points and 6 rebounds. But even if we had played well, we couldn't have beaten this talented Pershing team.

The talent show was that Friday, and before I knew it, all ten of us—my boys and our girls— were on stage performing our song. I did the lead singing and Stan, Floyd, Denny and Kenny did the backup vocals and synchronized dancing. Those guys did a great job. The girls sat in chairs and smiled as we sang to them. We got a lot of freshman votes, but probably not many from the upperclassmen, so we didn't win. First and second place went to seniors, and third place went to a junior. We all had fun though.

And when I sang those words about my girl, it was more than just an act to get laughs and votes. I really felt that way about Teresa. She's my girl, and I don't consider or look at any other girls.

Our next basketball game was another non-league game against Farmington Harrison. They were no Detroit Pershing, but it still would be a tough game. Coach started Mark and Steve as the forwards. He really liked their toughness even though Mark wasn't that skilled with the basketball. He started Kenny and Stan at guard, and it wasn't just because of Barnes' attitude. Coach really liked Kenny's and Stan's speed, and the varsity coach wanted players with speed to be the ones developed so he could have them in a few years. I started at center.

We trailed 22-19 at the half. Kenny actually led the way with 7 points, and I followed with 6. We seemed to be playing well. McCoy and Whitman were ready as reserve guards, and Barnes never got off the bench.

When we came back out after half time, a man in a suit who the other players recognized as Barnes' father, an attorney, came over to speak to Coach Reese. We were warming up and couldn't hear the conversation, but we all saw him shaking his head and waving his arms as he walked away.

We didn't do well in the second half and ended up losing the game by 14 points. With 42 seconds left, Coach called Barnes' name, but Barnes never looked at him and didn't get up. He had refused to play when called.

Coach stuck with same rotation, with Barnes at the end of the bench, for the next three games. We really started playing better, and we won one of our games just before the Christmas break. Basketball actually started being fun when I played with Stan, Kenny, Mark and Steve. I was averaging 12 points a game, and I was usually playing against shorter players. There weren't many 6'4" players at the freshman level.

With much of my time spent with basketball, I knew I was probably neglecting my girlfriend. One day I was talking to Kenny in the hall, and he told me things were going really well with Kate. He said he left her notes in her locker to tell her how much he liked her, and yesterday he'd brought her a flower. At first I thought, *Come on, Kenny, you're trying too hard!* But then I started thinking about the Dr. Stone paper. What was I doing to make Teresa feel special?

I decided to write her a note and hand it to her so she could read it later.

My dear Teresa,
I haven't been a good boyfriend to you. I became a starter on the basketball team, and it kind of consumed me. Luckily we have a break

from basketball starting on Friday when we get out for Christmas vacation. I didn't mean to neglect you.

You're the most special girl to me. I think about you a lot.

I'm hoping I can make this up to you. I know you have to visit some relatives over break, but if you have time for me, I want to take you to Big Boy and go see a movie with you.

Yours, Tom

A few hours later there was a note in my locker. I did some deep breathing. Was this the breakup letter? I held it but couldn't open it. I went to class and kept it with me, still unopened. After school, before basketball practice, I finally decided to open it.

My dear sweet Tom,

I've had it rough this year with my mom's divorce and moving. I moved to a new school but became very popular having a boyfriend who was a star football player. Now my boyfriend is the star of the basketball team. My rough year has turned into my best year.

Watching you play basketball is special to me. I know it's been really hard on you making the adjustment to be the star player.

You never neglected me. You're the best boyfriend ever. When it's cold outside, I've got the month of May just like you sang me. I saw it in your eyes when you were singing that you really meant it.

I'm happy to spend any time I can with you. I would love to go to dinner and movie or I

would be happy just to sit on the picnic table with
you and look out at the lake as we talk.
    Yours Always, T

My eyes watered as I read it. I tucked the
note away because I had to get ready for basketball
practice, but I was glad I'd written to her. Even
though she didn't require much of me, I decided I
wanted to do more to make her feel special.

"Lean on me when you're not strong,
And I'll be your friend, I'll help you carry on.
For it won't be long,
'Til I'm going to need somebody to lean on."
— Bill Withers (1972)

Christmas Eve

I went in for the biopsy to determine if the mass in my uterus was cancerous or benign. I just told Tom I had a doctor's appointment so he wouldn't worry, but I decided to tell Guy the truth. He was very supportive and promised to help out any way he could.

A few days after the test, Dr. Hart called to set up an appointment. I was able to see her the following Monday. She told me it might be a good idea if I brought a family member with me, but I decided to go alone and not bother anyone else.

"Ms. Mochina, it's good to see you," she said when I settled in her office. "I have the results of your biopsy. We found that the growth was malignant, which means it's cancerous and will continue to grow if we don't perform surgery."

I started to tear up. Surgery sounded risky, but if the cancer continued to grow I would die and Tom would have to go live with my parents in the city. I took a deep breath. "Surgery scares me," I confessed.

"Thank you for sharing your feelings," the doctor said. "I can certainly understand your concerns. The surgery I would like you to consider is called a hysterectomy, which will remove your uterus."

"Remove my uterus! How long will I live?" I cried even more. "How will I be able to function? Will I still be able to, you know, be with a man?"

She smiled at me. "If we remove your uterus, you should be able to live a normal life. If we don't remove it and the cancer spreads, you may have just a few years. The surgery will result in you no longer having periods, and without a uterus, you will no longer be able to get pregnant and have a child. Were you planning on more children?"

"I wanted more children when I get married someday, but I'm happy that I was able to have one child. So, I won't be able to be with a man again?"

She smiled. "You'll still be able to function sexually, but you won't be able to have more children. I know this is a big decision. Would you like to talk to family members before deciding?"

"Who will do the surgery?"

"I will."

"Dr. Hart, my son will graduate from high school in four years. Although I might want other children, I need to be there for the son I have, and I might not if I don't have surgery, right?"

"I would highly recommend the surgery if you want to see your son graduate."

"Then I'd like to schedule it."

I scheduled the surgery for January. I knew I had to tell my mother and father, and I needed to tell Guy too. But I decided I wanted to talk to Gramps first to see what he thought.

On Saturday, I walked down to his house to sit on his picnic table, but he was outside and saw me as I approached.

"Eve, my beautiful neighbor. How good to see you."

"Hi, Gramps. I really wanted to talk to you. I've been seeing Dr. Hart, and she's determined that I need a hysterectomy to remove my uterus due to cancer. What do you think?"

"Oh, I'm so sorry to hear this. How can I help?"

"She told me that I should have the surgery or I might die. So I have to have it, right?"

"I trust Dr. Hart. She's a great gynecologist. What are your concerns about the surgery?"

"Is there a chance they could put me to sleep and I would never wake up?"

"I remember Tom had to have anesthesia when he got his teeth pulled, and he woke up. I think there's an excellent chance you'll wake up and make a full recovery."

"I need to tell Guy that I won't be able to have more children. Guy loves children. What if he decides to leave me?

"Luckily, you already have three children between the two of you. If it's important for Guy to have another child and he's going to leave you, it would probably be better to find that out now. Do you really want to get married to a man who doesn't accept you and your health conditions?"

I nodded in agreement.

"What do you think about telling Tom?" I asked.

"There's no need to tell him until a few days before surgery," Gramps said. "There's nothing he can do to help, but he may worry. I would wait to tell him."

"Thanks, Gramps." We talked for a few more minutes, and then I smiled and walked back home.

I called Guy and told him we needed to talk about something very important, and I drove out to Dearborn on Sunday afternoon. While the kids played, I told him about the upcoming surgery and that I would no longer be able to have children. He was very supportive.

"Eve, if the two of us ever had a child, it would be wonderful. But I understand that isn't going to happen. I want you to live a long life, and I want you to be my girlfriend. Nothing changes between us just because you're having surgery."

I just looked at how handsome and sweet he was and hugged him.

The following Sunday, the day came for my quartet's performance of "The Hallelujah Chorus" at the church. I sang it with another lady and two men. We had rehearsed together, and it really sounded pretty good, but when I'd agreed to sing this, I didn't know I had cancer.

Guy brought his kids all the way from Dearborn to watch me, and Gramps and his wife were there as usual. Tom was also there, and I could tell how proud he was of me performing the song.

After church, we all played at my house. I watched Tom play with Carl and Karen. He was so patient with them. Tom's girlfriend Teresa came over and played with the kids as well. At one point we all went outside and built a big snowman. It took both Tom and Guy to roll the big base and lift up the midsection. Teresa and I put on the finishing touches with a scarf, a carrot nose and a couple of pieces of charcoal for the eyes. All of the kids made snow angels.

Afterward we all got cleaned up and Guy took us to Big Boy. At dinner, we discussed Christmas. Guy was going to let his kids go over to their grandparents' for a while on Christmas Eve and then go get them so they could wake up on Christmas morning at their own house. He wanted to come out on Christmas Eve to celebrate with Tom and me. I warned him that I didn't have a lot of money to buy gifts, and he told me he didn't want anything from me but a smile.

Guy came out to the house on Christmas Eve, and I made him and Tom ham, green beans and some make-believe potatoes.

After lunch, Guy said, "I see some presents under that tree. I wonder what could be in this really big box? Oh, it says *To Tom*."

"Wow! Can I open it?" asked Tom looking at me and Guy.

We nodded, and Tom ripped the paper off to find an acoustic guitar in a case.

"Oh, Bernie, thanks so much. I've played Teresa's a lot, but now I have my very own guitar. We can play duets. Can I try it?"

"Tom, first let's give Bernie his present," I suggested.

Tom handed Guy the present, and he opened it to find a light blue dress shirt and wide paisley tie.

"Thanks. How'd you guys know I needed a new mod tie? This is great. All right, Tom, you can play guitar now. Eve, would you take a walk with me down to the docks?"

"What? You got me a new boat?"

He smiled. "If I did get you a boat, it wouldn't be in the water because the lake is frozen."

We bundled up and walked to the docks, leaving Tom behind to play his guitar. When we got there, we noticed the docks and row boats were all on shore, and all of the motor boats were gone. The lake was frozen over.

"Eve, would you walk with me out to where my boat normally is in the summer?"

"Is it safe to walk on the ice?"

"I'll be with you."

We walked out on the frozen lake to approximately where Guy's boat was docked in the summer.

"Eve, this is the place where I first laid eyes on you and knew I wanted you to be my special lady. Seven months later, I look at you and still want you to be with me. This is our special spot."

He was so sweet, I wanted to cry, but I didn't want my tears to freeze to my face. He then got down on one knee.

"Eve, I know we've had our ups and downs. But every time I'm away from you, I can't wait to see you again. Our lives are complicated. We're both parents. We're not two people, we're five."

He pulled out a small box and opened it, showing me a diamond ring.

"Guy!" I screamed.

"Eve, I'm asking you to be my wife. I want to grow old with you and hold you every day. Would you be my wife?"

"Oh, yes, yes, yes." I hugged him and cried, right out on the frozen lake. When I finally composed myself, I tried the ring on and it was too big.

"I'll take you to the jeweler after Christmas and get it sized correctly," Guy promised.

We walked back to the house, where Tom was still busy playing his new guitar. He didn't even ask about our walk.

After Guy left, Tom and I celebrated Christmas Eve together.

"Mom, is that a new ring?" he asked.

"Yes," I told him. "We didn't want to disturb your guitar playing when we got back, but Guy, um, Bernie gave me the ring."

Tom looked at it. "Does this mean he wants to marry you and be my stepfather?"

"Yes."

Tom was quiet for a moment before he looked at me. "Bernie's a great guy," he said. "I'd be honored."

"Oh, Tom, that means so much to me." I have him a big hug.

A couple weeks later, a few days before my surgery, I told Tom I was going to have to be in the hospital for a few days and that Bernie was going to come out and stay at the house with him.

"Is everything okay?"

"Yes. I just need to be in the hospital until Sunday so I heal from my surgery. Bernie took

Thursday and Friday off work. He's going to stay with me during the surgery on Thursday and then come get you from basketball practice and bring you out to the hospital to have dinner with me."

Tom seemed to understand, and although he looked concerned, he didn't appear to worry that much. I knew he was still going through a lot with the basketball team and was probably distracted.

On Thursday, Bernie picked me up and took me to Farmington where we met Dr. Hart. Although I was very scared, I let them put me to sleep.

Later I opened my eyes and Guy was sitting there. I looked at him and didn't say anything. He just looked at me for a few minutes.

"There are the beautiful eyes I've been waiting for."

"Am I okay?"

"Eve, you're marvelous. Dr. Hart said everything went well."

"Where's Tom?"

Guy smiled. "He's still at school. I'm going to pick him up after basketball practice."

I went back to sleep, and a few hours later, Guy went to pick up Tom. It was great to see my son when they returned.

"Tom, I won't be able to cook you dinner tonight," I told him with a laugh.

"I know, Mom. Bernie and I stopped at McDonald's. Hey, what nice flowers!"

"I saw those come in but I haven't been able to read the card."

Tom went over and checked. "They're from Gramps and Ruth Davis!"

"Oh, how sweet!"

I spent my three nights in the hospital, and on Sunday I got to go home. I was still moving a little slowly but I had work on Monday.

"I say to myself, you're such a lucky guy,
To have a girl like her is truly a dream come true.
Out of all the fellas in the world, she belongs to me."
— *The Temptations (1971)*

Making Amends

T he big news on New Year's Day was that Roberto Clemente, the great Puerto Rican baseball player, had died in a plane crash. This was just terrible and very sad. I'd still never been in a plane, and every time I heard news like this, I feared airplanes even more.

"Mom, have you decided on a date for the wedding?"

"Yes, Tom. Bernie and I are getting married on May twenty-sixth. It's the Saturday of Memorial Day weekend. We met on Memorial Day weekend, so it will be special. It's also close to the last day of school and the end of baseball."

"Where are we going to live?"

"We haven't talked a lot about this. Bernie has a house in Dearborn, so that's an option."

"I have to work seven days a week for Gramps again this summer, so I couldn't live in Dearborn," I told her, feeling a little panicked.

"I know you want to work this summer."

"I still have three years of high school at Walled Lake Central too. How's that going to work?"

"Tom I really don't know," my mother told me. "I've been without a husband for fifteen years, and now I have the chance to get married to a wonderful man. You may have to make some sacrifices. With Bernie, you'll have a much nicer house, a garage and a shower."

"I understand, Mom. But I have my girlfriend here, some great friends, and this is where I play baseball, football and basketball. I can't leave."

"I'll talk to Bernie about your concerns," she promised.

"Let me state again that I'm *not* moving to Dearborn," I told her.

It had been fun being off for Christmas break, but I was not too sorry when it was time to go back to school. I was excited to get back into basketball.

After the first day back, I got dressed and came out to warm up for practice. Barnes walked up to me.

"Tom, can we talk a minute?"

I looked at him for a few seconds and then said, "Sure." He'd never called me Tom before.

We walked over toward the bench area.

"This has been a rough season," he told me. "I came in thinking this was my team to lead and that the guys I'd played with before would continue to be the starters. I didn't anticipate a few of the guys not starting and I certainly never imagined that I wouldn't start. Now I find myself in a position where I'm not even getting bench minutes. I want to get back to where I can be a strong contributor even though this is your team now."

I shook my head a little. "This is not my team. I play a role. I try to play defense, get some rebounds, and score on the block. This is Coach Reese's team and I'm grateful to be a part of it. You purposely threw bad passes to sabotage this team."

"I know. I'm sorry. I want you to give me another chance. I have the best ball-handling skills on the team, and I can contribute if we work together."

"You want me to work with you after the way you've acted?"

"Yes. I said I made a mistake, and I'm sorry."

"I'll forgive you, but let me ask you this: Did you ever watch Batman?"

"Of course."

"What would Batman do if the Joker approached him and said he was sorry and wanted to start working together?"

"It's the Joker. He would never trust that he was telling the truth."

I just looked at him. "It's Coach Reese's team. He can play whatever guards he wants, but I'm very comfortable with Stan and Kenny. They've never purposely thrown me bad passes."

Barnes just shrugged, and we went over to warm up. After a few minutes, Coach Reese called me over.

"Did Barnes apologize to you?"

"He did."

"I asked him to apologize before I started working him back in to the rotation."

"It sounded like he only did it because you asked him to. I'm sure the Joker would apologize to Batman if Chief O'Hara would let him out of jail. We'll see how it goes."

Coach Reese looked at me, seeming to think about the analogy. Then he told me to continue warming up.

We ran a lot of drills, and then set up the scrimmage. The starters—Stan, Kenny, Mark, Steve and me—wore yellow shirts, and Barnes and Larry also wore yellow shirts to sub in. The other five guys wore blue.

The scrimmage went well, and Barnes certainly played like he was trying to get his job back. All of his passes to me were very good. Larry looked good too when he filled in. But McCoy and Herring, who had been starters for the last two years, seemed to still be out of the rotation.

Our lunch table was getting bigger. Besides Stan, Denny and Floyd, Mark and Kenny were now my daily lunch pals. And Steve and Larry had also joined us. We joked around every day and had fun.

The girls sat together and had their fun at lunch too. One day I was late, and it didn't look like the boys had saved me a seat, so I sat down with the girls, who playfully accepted me at their table. Then I heard Mark yell over that they had a seat for me, so I went back to the guys.

Barnes, McCoy and Herring usually sat together, but not with us, and it seemed Whitman, Jalkanen and Brown had become friends, so they sat together at lunch as well. None of these six guys played baseball or football, but many of them were golfers or tennis players. In fact, McCoy and Whitman were two of the top tennis players in our class, and Brown and Barnes were the two top golfers. I had never tried these rich-kid sports.

Our first game back after Christmas break was against Farmington. Coach Reese used the same starting lineup he'd used in practice and subbed in Barnes for the guards, Larry for the forwards and Herring now backed up me at center.

Kenny played well and scored ten points in the first half. I had six points, and Barnes had six points off the bench. Everyone who played scored except for Stan, who played good defense. We led at the half 35-26.

Farmington came out in the second half and scored the first six points. Coach subbed in Barnes and Larry for Stan and Mark. The score stayed close. Starting the fourth quarter, we only led by one point. Kenny and I took a seat on the bench to get some rest, and when I looked out on the floor, the lineup was now the starting lineup used in the seventh and eighth grades. I was curious to see how they'd do, and they didn't do that badly, but with five minutes left in the game, we were trailing by five points, so Coach put Kenny, Mark and me back in to play with Barnes and Steve. I can only assume that this was the lineup Coach thought gave him the best chance to win.

The first time down, Mark set the screen for me, and I hustled to the right block. Barnes made a good pass, and I was able to put it in and also got fouled. I hit the free throw, and we were now down by only two points.

With forty seconds left, we led by two points, and we just had to play tough defense to win. But with fifteen seconds left, one of their players hit a fifteen-foot jump shot, and they tied us.

Coach called time out and set up a play. He wanted Barnes to bring it up and me to help set a pick, if needed at half court, and then hustle to the left block. He then wanted a pick and roll with Barnes and Steve.

As expected, Farmington pressed full court. I got a good screen on Barnes' man, who then had to chase after him. Steve set the next screen, but Barnes' man was not right with him so he rolled to the basket. The man guarding Steve came over to stop Barnes, and Barnes threw a pass around the defender to Steve, who laid it up and in. We won with me in the process of heading to the rim in case Steve missed for the put back.

It was an exciting win, and we actually walked off the floor for the first time looking like a team. We executed the play, Barnes actually threw a good pass, and we all celebrated the win together.

Coach Reese joined us in the locker room. "Who are you guys? Before Christmas I thought I had a bunch of individuals who couldn't be a team. Now it looks like I've got a team who wants to challenge for the conference title. Nice work."

On Friday night, the group of us who ate lunch together and a group of girls decided to meet at the varsity basketball game. The varsity team was really good. We had a six-foot-nine player who was all-state and being recruited by about every college imaginable. He was amazing to watch. He had long, blond, straight hair parted down the middle that fell to his shoulders. He could handle the ball, and he was a great shooter. He also had incredible athletic ability. He was putting on a show one time at practice and, with a running start, set a quarter on the top of the backboard. He then joked that anyone who wanted his quarter could jump up and get it, but of course no one could. The other varsity starters were really good too, and the team rarely lost.

Shelley, Teresa's friend from her old school and Stan's homecoming date, came out for the weekend to stay with Teresa, and Teresa's mother picked up Stan and me to take us to the game.

It was good to spend time with Teresa. I listened to her talk about what she had going on in her life as I watched the game. And Stan was really excited to see Shelley. I rarely see him with girls, but he just lights up when she's around.

Shelley told us her mother might move to this area after school was out if she could find a place. Teresa was really excited about that possibility. Stan told us his parents were getting along much better, and they might stay together.

I still didn't know my status. With my mom getting married, what would happen to me? It seemed like all of my friends had worked things out so they could stay at Walled Lake Central, and now Shelley might be moving here too. I couldn't imagine moving to Dearborn. I loved my mother and Bernie was great, but somehow I needed to stay in the area.

Who could I live with? I couldn't really live with any of my friends. But I knew Gramps would take me. Maybe I should talk to Gramps. I decided to not say a whole lot more about my situation to avoid worrying my friends.

As expected, the varsity team had another huge win, and the all-state player scored 35 points with 15 rebounds. At the end of the game, being up big, he saw his replacement at the scorer's table.

He got the ball and went hard to the basket, slam-dunking the basketball hard into the hoop. The crowd stood and cheered.

In 1973, it was considered a technical foul if you slam dunked, but since the team was guaranteed a win, he gladly accepted the technical and no basket to excite the crowd.

When the game was over, Stan's mom and dad came to get us, and they took us to The Little Brown Jug. It was the first time I'd ever been in a bar. My mother doesn't drink, so I really hadn't ever been around people drinking beer. It was entertaining. Stan, Shelley, Teresa and I all ordered root beer, but we joked and called it beer. Stan's parents bought us pizza.

The next day I headed down to look for Gramps. He was out plowing some snow.

"Tommy Boy, I was hoping you'd be down so I shoveled my deck and got the snow off the chairs. We can sit out and pretend it's summer. Do you know how to catch a bear?"

"I do. You've told me this one. You cut a hole in the ice and put peas around it. When the bear comes to take a pea, you kick him in."

"Tom you're close. When the bear comes to take a pea, you kick him in the ice hole."

I started laughing. Now I got the whole joke.

"Gramps, I have good news and bad news."

"Have you told me this one before?

"No, I'm serious. My mother is getting married."

"I heard that. Bernie's a great guy. They both are really lucky. Now, is that the good news or the bad news?"

"Both. I like Bernie. I really believe we can be a family with him and his two children. The bad news is that his house is in Dearborn. My job is here. You're here. My girlfriend's here. My friends are here. I really want to continue to play sports with my friends at Walled Lake Central."

"This is a tough situation," said Gramps.

"I talked to my mom, and she's getting stressed out about it too. I get the feeling she might even call off the marriage for me. I don't want her to do that, but I don't want to move to Dearborn. I wish I could come live with you."

"As much as I'd be happy to take you in, you have to live with your mother. She's so good to you. She would not be happy if you lived with someone else. Have her stop down some time, and I'll talk with her."

"Thanks, Gramps."

"Now, Tom, I have some sad news."

I looked at Gramps intently. "You're okay, aren't you?"

"I'm a tough old goat. It's going to take a lot to bring me down. But I got a call from George who said you'd know him as George of the Jungle?"

"Yes, is he okay?"

"Well, George's best friend, George, was killed in a car accident on New Year's Eve."

"What? George? The guy we called Ape? I can't believe that."

"I'm really sorry, Tom."

The news stunned me. He was so strong. He was so young. What really got to me was the

185

memory of him yelling that he could have been killed. Talk about a guy who really wanted to live! He was devastated that he could have been killed last summer. This was very sad news.

We had three more basketball games, and we won two of them. We were really starting to play well. We were now four wins with five losses for the season. Barnes was still coming off the bench with Larry, but they were playing significant minutes. And McCoy and Herring were getting time too. Stan was still starting, but his minutes were dropping. I'm happy to say I continued to play well with any combination of players Coach Reese put in the game.

"I know I saw Miss Lucy.
Down along the tracks.
She lost her home and her family.
And she won't be coming back.
Without Love, where would you be now?"
— *The Doobie Brothers (1973)*

I Love Lucy

I'm living the dream working at the Detroit Free Press. It was everything I hoped it would be. I was writing the articles I wanted, and the people of Michigan were reading them. I loved being back in the state where I grew up.

I'd spent two weeks living at my mom's, and now I'm living for two weeks at my dad's house. It's been great spending time with them, and I've really enjoyed spending time with my brother and sister and getting together with friends from the area. But I'll be glad when I get moved into my own place with Mark.

He and I have been getting along well. I think we were both able to change the bad habits we got into prior to last summer. We've been following Dr. Stone's paper and are really trying to communicate and understand each other.

We bought a house in Northville, which is a suburb outside Detroit with easy access to the highways for both of us to go to work. It's a four-bedroom house with a two-car garage. The best part is the big backyard.

We had looked in Dearborn to be closer to work, but it just felt like the city to us, and Northville is so much closer to my mom and dad.

We've decided to get married on March 24. We're closing on the house on March 1, and Mark is going to move in. I'm choosing to be traditional and not move in with him until after we're married.

We met with the minister who's going to officiate our wedding, and we all agreed that Mark and I share the same religious values and faith. We also agreed on how to raise our future children in the church. We only needed one meeting with him, and he said he felt good about our chances for a long relationship.

We also agreed to meet with Dr. Stone for premarital counseling. We're both comfortable with her, and she helped us a lot last summer.

So on Thursday, we met with Dr. Stone—only this time at her Michigan office.

"Good to see you both again. I'm so glad you decided to stay together and get married."

After exchanging greetings, she asked us if we remembered the interaction scale in her paper. We both did. Then she asked us to rate where we were on the scale.

"Ten," said Mark.

"I would say eight. But I think eight is ahead of most couples getting married, and I want to leave some room to grow for a nine or ten someday. The true test'll be when we start living in the same house together."

Mark agreed to the score of eight.

"If you can make it your entire lives and have a score of eight, that would be exceptional," said Dr. Stone. "However, eight is where you are today. For the first year of your marriage, I want you to record your interaction score on the first of every month. In the second year, you should do this every quarter. After that, once a year would be fine as long as you're at a score of six or above. If you fall below six, go back to every month and do the things you need to do to get back to a six or higher. If you continue to maintain a score of six or higher, then you can go back to once a year. If you drop below a two, you may want to consider calling me or another counselor to help you get your score back up."

Mark and I both agreed to this plan.

"How're you going to make decisions when you don't agree?" Dr. Stone asked.

Mark and I looked at each other and didn't have an answer.

"I want you to take that question as homework and let's talk about it next week," suggested Dr. Stone. "The next question is important since you're both back in Michigan. Your parents live in Michigan?" she said, looking at me.

I nodded.

"And, Mark, your parents are in Chicago, right?"

He nodded. "Yes, in Joliet just outside of Chicago."

"Your second homework question is to decide how much influence your parents will have on your life or if you'll make decisions just between the two of you. My third question for homework is how you're going to handle things when the unexpected happens—one of you loses your job, one of you has an illness, or someone close to you dies. Talk about what you're going to do in a crisis situation, and we'll discuss next time."

We agreed.

"The last thing I'd like the two of you to do is decide on some boundaries, so I've provided a list of things for you to consider. Do you have time to complete these items by next Thursday? Could you each commit to blocking off three hours to discuss these topics?

"Mark, do you want to meet Saturday morning at my dad's house?" I asked him. "I'll tell him what we're doing, and I'm sure he'll give us the time."

"Sure, I'll see you then," said Mark, and then he looked at Dr. Stone. "I can make it next week."

I told Dr. Stone I could make it next week as well.

We'd agreed to meet at 9:30, and on Saturday, Mark arrived at 9:24. I still felt a little bad that he always came early now. These days I really would cut him some slack if he were late.

My dad and Ruth went shopping, even though he tried to tell me he should stay and mediate. My dad is such the joker.

Mark and I each got a cup of coffee and started to tackle the questions. We pondered the first question about decision making. For routine decisions like what we're having for dinner, we agreed that Mark would get his way 40% and I would get 60% of the time. The paper recommended those percentages based on Dr. Stone's experience with happy couples.

We then discussed who would take care of the finances and how our accounts would be combined. We decided for now, with both of us working, that I would control the finances and checking account. We would combine all but 10% of our income, and we would each maintain our own account with the extra 10% to do with as we pleased. We also agreed that we should try to save some money while we were both working.

We then discussed decisions about medical care for the future children, and I agreed to be in charge of that. We also discussed discipline for our future children. We agreed to talk how we would deal with child problems as they arose, but that Mark would be the ultimate decision-maker on that one.

We talked about who would make a decision in an absolute crisis situation and agreed that Mark would have that one as well. We discussed how we would support each other in a crisis, and we decided that if one of us lost our job, our health, someone close to us or another type of loss, we would continue to love and support each other through the tough times.

The question about parent involvement was an easy one. We both planned to listen to our parents, but we would be the ultimate decision makers. I wondered if some couples still felt controlled by their parents at age thirty or forty.

We next tackled the boundaries questions. Our first idea was that we would never tell the other person we didn't love them, no matter how bad things got. We also decided we would never tell the other person to *get out*. Our next boundary was that we would not physically harm each other.

The next set of boundaries related to health. We both said if we started to gain weight, we would go on a diet. We agreed to no smoking and no drug use. We both agreed to drinking alcohol in moderation, and we both agreed to exercise three times a week.

The next discussion item on the boundary list was about attending worship services. We figured we would attend at least thirty times a year.

We talked about going out with friends without our spouse. We agreed that we would discuss if needed, but once a month didn't sound unreasonable.

We were surprised to see honesty on the list. Without much thought, we committed to always be honest, and said that if it was ever discovered that one of us had lied, we would have a serious conversation about it.

The next item was that each of us be faithful, and we overwhelmingly agreed.

Forgiveness was next on the list. We committed to forgive each other for mistakes as long as they weren't related to honesty or faithfulness.

The next boundary was the 30-day rule about not bringing up events that had happened more than thirty days ago for the purpose of hurting the other person. We both knew this would be very important and said we'd try hard to make this a reality.

The next several boundaries were easy to agree to because they were all from Dr. Stone's paper. We'd spend time making sure we knew how the other was doing every day. We'd understand, appreciate and accept each other. We'd be consistent in our greetings and rituals. We'd share fondness for the other. We'd strive to assume the positive intentions of the other. We'd throw good passes, and we'd strive to manage conflict when it arose.

We got through the list with only two cups of coffee each. We felt very accomplished, and decided we'd worked hard enough and should go to Bill Knapp's for lunch in Farmington.

When we attended the session the following Thursday, Dr. Stone wanted to know our positive interaction score, and we agreed it was still an eight. We went through our answers to her questions, and she told us how well we'd done. We scheduled one more appointment for two weeks before the wedding.

The time flew, and at our final appointment, we agreed we were still at an eight and were doing well. Dr. Stone asked us what we'd learned about arguing.

"Arguing is very unproductive. A lot of people try to spend time trying to prove themselves right and the other wrong. Really there is no right and wrong," said Mark.

"I agree. There's no right or wrong. It's just two people think differently and we should accept and appreciate this difference and really try to understand the other person," I said.

"People argue all the time, but they don't stop to think that trying to prove themselves right is only trying to prove the person they love wrong," commented Mark.

"And one last thing to mention is that arguing only creates very bad memories and it is hard to overcome damage to relationships. I'm committed to really trying to not argue," I said.

"I am too," he said.

"It sounds like you two are on the right track. Any last thoughts about what you learned in therapy," asked Dr. Stone.

"I learned that we're both really committed to a happy marriage," I said.

Then she turned to Mark.

"I learned what I have known for a long time," he said. "I love Lucy!"

"Knock, knock, knockin' on Heaven's door.
Knock, knock, knockin' on Heaven's door.
Knock, knock, knockin' on Heaven's door.
Knock, knock, knockin' on Heaven's door."
— Bob Dylan (1972)

Strangle Hold

For our next basketball game, we traveled to Waterford Township. We'd heard they had a reputation for playing dirty, but we would never have guessed what was about to happen.

We led 34-24 at the half, and I was having a big game with 17 points. Barnes had started but got into foul trouble, so Coach started Stan in the second half along with Mark, Steve, Kenny and me.

The first time we went on offense, I was able to score off a Mark screen and post up off the right block. We were also playing good defense and making it tough for Waterford to score.

The next time down the court, I ran to set up for offense down on the block and was looking at Kenny bringing the ball up. All of a sudden, I felt hands around my neck from behind, followed by squeezing. I gasped for breath, growled and tried to break free.

I saw Mark come over and punch the guy in the side, and his hands broke free. Stan hurried over too and punched the guy in the face. I'd never seen Stan punch anyone.

I was still gasping for air, but walked toward the guy with a mean look on my face. I had thoughts of kicking him in the face, but I held back. I felt a shove on my back and turned around to see a player from Waterford.

"What's your problem? What's wrong with you people? You just pushed the wrong guy," I yelled.

Coach Reese appeared on the scene and told us to get to our bench. The Waterford team went to their bench too while the coaches and referees talked.

Mark sat on one side of me and Stan the other.

Mark said, "I was looking to come set the pick for you and noticed a Waterford player at the drinking fountain, but he wasn't one of the five in the game. Then I saw him come up on you and try to strangle you. I got there as quick as I could. Sorry, man."

"I saw that guy's hands on your neck and I turned red," Stan added. "I just let my natural reaction happen. All I could see was that the guy was trying to kill you. I don't normally hit anyone, but if my best friend's in danger, look out."

"I appreciate it, guys. Wow, that really scared me. I still feel I'm gasping for breath."

Coach Reese came back to the bench. "Franciszek and Nelson have been ejected from the game."

"What? And is their whole team ejected including the coach who put them up to this?" I asked.

"No one on their team got ejected," said Coach Reese. "What did the coach do?"

"The coach sent a player, number fifteen, who wasn't in the game, to get a drink and then to try to strangle Tom. Also, number forty-five needs to be ejected for pushing Tom. I want them all ejected," said Mark.

"I agree," Kenny said. If those three aren't ejected, I'm not going back in."

Steve and Larry both said they wouldn't play either.

Then Barnes said, "I'm with the rest of these guys. This is unfair. They assaulted a teammate, and we get punished. I'm out too."

We were all surprised that Barnes had joined us.

Coach Reese looked at us and then walked back to the referee. They talked for a minute and then we heard Coach say, "I want those guys out and you to allow all of my players to play or we're getting on the bus and leaving."

The referee walked back to talk to the other coach who had already put his players back on the floor. After a moment he came back and told Coach Reese that the other team denied anything remotely like that.

Coach Reese just looked at us and shook his head. We all got up and left the gym. I'm not sure I could've played anyway because I was still very upset. I had to process the idea that at any time someone could come up from behind and try to seriously harm me.

However, on the way home, I think we really bonded as a team. There were no more yours versus ours and there was no longer an *I* in *team*. We were ready to make a run at the conference championship.

When I got home, I told my mother what had happened, and she was very upset. I almost wished I hadn't told her. Somehow, she thought it was because I was Hungarian or didn't live with a father, but the other team didn't know me. I tried to tell her those things had nothing to do with it.

Although I believe the game was recorded as a loss due to forfeiting, we counted the game as a win, and we were now five and five. At practice the next day, our coach told us the varsity coach was talking to the league about the incident.

That weekend I went over to Teresa's to hang out. I brought my guitar, and she continued to show me how to play some songs. I was still nowhere near the guitar player she was, but I kept trying. And I could still sing any of the songs.

After we played for a while, we watched some TV and cuddled close together. She started rubbing my chest, and I got really uncomfortable because her fingers were getting close to my throat. I grabbed her hand and took it off my chest.

"Hey, what's going on?" she asked. "You don't like me rubbing you?"

"I like you rubbing me, but your fingers were too close to my neck. It makes me uncomfortable."

"I'd never hurt you. You're my big, strong, handsome boyfriend."

"I know, and you're my sweet, beautiful girlfriend but I just got really uncomfortable thinking your fingers might touch my neck."

She didn't understand. I'm not sure I did either. She took it as a criticism of her.

"I'll just sit over here," she said, and she got up and moved.

It's not that my neck was so sore, but for some reason I just didn't want anyone near it.

After I left Teresa's house, I stopped down and looked for Gramps.

"Tom, my deck is clear of snow," he called. "Come on over."

"Did you hear about the Waterford game?" I asked him.

"Yes. I'm glad you're okay. It's hard to believe a coach would allow that to happen. How are you dealing with it?"

"Not well. I can't take my mind off my neck when I'm trying to play basketball. I keep thinking someone will grab me. In practice, Tom Brown, one of my teammates, touched my neck, and I turned and stared him down, thinking about punching him. I know he was just doing his best to play and didn't mean to harm me. But I'm not the player I used to be because I can't get this incident out of my mind. I thought it was just basketball, but earlier today I got really uncomfortable with Teresa getting to close to my neck."

"You had a very bad experience. I can understand why you would be cautious about your neck."

"What do you suggest?"

"Well, outside of basketball, you need to explain to your friends that you went through a trauma, and it would help if they didn't touch your neck until you're able to deal with it. Basketball is another story. If you tell the opponents you don't want your neck touched, they'll purposely try to touch it."

"I know they would," I agreed. "So what can I do to play basketball?"

"You might want to take a couple games off until you feel safe playing again."

"I can't do that. We have two big league games coming up against Livonia Stevenson and Pontiac Northern."

"Do you feel safe playing against those teams?"

"Safe? Hopefully they don't feel safe playing against me," I said with a big smile.

"Your safety on the court has been compromised. You have to believe no one will try to strangle you again. If it does happen, you can deal with it then.

"If this happens again, I'm sticking with baseball and football."

"If someone touches your neck, you won't like it, but you have to tell yourself that they're just playing basketball and not trying to club you to death with a baseball bat. Can you think that?"

"I'll give it try."

On Sunday, I went over to Teresa's again. "I want you to touch my neck," I told her.

"What?"

"Please. I know you won't try to hurt me. I'm trying to process the trauma of the strangle hold, and I need the exposure of having it touched. Just rub it gently."

She touched and rubbed my neck and throat area. "Are you okay?"

"I'm good. I have to use thinking strategies to allow you to do this, but I can do it. Will you be patient with me for a while?"

She smiled and we played some guitar together.

—◆—

The next day at practice I talked to the coach. I told him about the troubles I'd been having and that I was working through them and really wanting to play against Stevenson. He seemed to understand. I could tell he really wanted me to play in this game.

We came out with the starting lineup of Barnes, Kenny, Mark, Steve and me. About halfway through the quarter, he put in Herring for me, and I came to the bench.

"Tom, you're not getting open on the block. Why can't you get through the screen? You're a big part of our offense. I need you to get open. Are Mark and Steve not setting the pick?"

"They are. I'll work harder."

"Good, rest up. You're going back to start the second quarter."

I realized I was tentative out there and wasn't helping the team. If I continued, we weren't going to beat Livonia Stevenson. We trailed 14-6 at the end of the first quarter.

The first time down the court to start the second quarter, I fought through and got my position on the block. McCoy, who had come in for Barnes, got me the ball, and I turned and scored. We ran the same play the next time down, and I scored again. We went to the well a third time, and this time the opponent fouled me hard. I quickly used my thinking strategy. I told myself he was just frustrated that I'd scored. I made one of two free throws, so we trailed 16-11. After that I had a couple blocked shots on the defensive end of the floor, which helped us get back in it. And Kenny got a couple fast break layups. We trailed at halftime 24-23.

We trailed 44-43 with 30 seconds left, and Coach Reese called time. His play was to post me up on the right block and have Barnes feed me the ball.

"Tom, go up strong because they're going to foul you. Can you do it?"

I looked at Coach and nodded. I was determined to do this.

We ran the play, and Barnes got me the ball. I turned and jumped and felt the foul, but I was so close I was almost able to drop the ball in the basket. I got the basket but missed the free throw.

We were up by one, so we wanted to play tough defense but not foul. Kenny's man took about a 21-foot jump shot with Kenny's hand in his face. Steve secured the rebound, and we had beaten Livonia Stevenson in a close game.

It wasn't going to get easier. Our next game was against Pontiac Northern, an all-black school. They were undefeated in conference play and had only lost to their crosstown rival, Pontiac Central.

The first quarter ended with us leading 18-17. They weren't stopping us, but they were beating us down the floor and getting uncontested layups. Stan didn't play against Livonia as Barnes, McCoy and Kenny all played well at the guards, but Coach Reese called Stan over and put him in the second quarter.

"I don't care if you don't score one point. Your job is to hound Washington and not let him get any more open layups. Can you do it? Kenny, you hound Russell and don't let him get layups."

Coach's plan worked, and we led at the half 32-27. Coach stuck with the plan in the second half but subbed Barnes in some. We led 60-57 with 28 seconds left.

Pontiac Northern had the ball, and Kenny's man brought it up the court. Kenny did all he could to make it tough. When he got the ball to the top of the key, he turned and threw it to the other guard, whom Stan was guarding. Stan stepped in, caught the ball and dribbled it as fast as he could the other way. I sprinted as fast as I could after Stan, and the Northern guards were also in hot pursuit.

Seeing Stan was in trouble, I said "trailer," and Stan flipped the ball high over his shoulder, only hearing my voice, not seeing me. I jumped and caught the ball and was able to drop it in a foot from the basket. So we beat Pontiac Northern 62-57.

After the game, everyone was talking about Stan's steal and his no-look pass to me. I was really happy for Stan after he hadn't played in the Livonia game.

.

"Whenever you call me, I'll be there.
Whenever you want me, I'll be there.
Whenever you need me, I'll be there.
I'll be around."
— The Spinners (1972)

Jolly Roger

I woke up Saturday morning and was all excited for my trip to Indianapolis with Stan and Louise. "Everyone ready to go?" I asked after breakfast.

Stan helped me carry the suitcases to the car and we started off on the drive.

"This is so nice of the Indianapolis Indians organization to honor former players," said Louise.

"Dad, this is so cool. They're going to have Ernie Harwell there to lead the ceremonies?" added Stan.

"I heard he'll be there and allow us to take pictures with him," I said. Ernie was the radio voice of the Detroit Tigers.

"How'd you get them to let Tom sing the national anthem?"

"When they invited me, I asked who was going to sing it and told them I knew a really good 14-year-old singer. They told me if I could get him to come, he could sing."

"That's really far out!"

"Tom is coming with his mom and Bernie," I said.

"I know, and Shelley and Teresa are coming down with Teresa's mom. Hey, Dad, did anyone ever famous play for Indianapolis?"

"Well, let's start with Grover Cleveland Alexander."

"The president?"

"No, no, that's Grover Cleveland. This guy was a pitcher who went on to the majors. Ever heard of Luke Appling, the White Sox shortstop? He was a former Indianapolis Indian. Let's see...we can add Harmon Killebrew, Pete Rose, Rocky Colavito, Roger Maris, and Bob Uecker to the list. I played with all of those guys."

"Wow, some impressive names!" exclaimed Stan.

"Yes, one year Maris was my backup, and a few years later, he was hitting sixty-one homeruns for the Yankees. I often wish I could have another chance. It was so close to being me playing right field next to Mickey Mantle."

When we got to Indy, we checked into the hotel and then drove to Victory Field, which had been renamed Bush Stadium since I'd played there. Stan and Louise went up to the seats to wait for the others while I went into the locker room.

I met a bunch of former Indians. There were only a few I'd actually met previously.

"Hi, I'm Roger," I said, introducing myself over and over again.

Then a man walked up to me, and I immediately recognized him as Ernie Harwell. "Hi, I'm Ernie."

"Ernie, of course I know who you are. It's an honor. Roger Franciszek."

"Roger, it's such a pleasure to meet you. Thank you for inviting me. I just couldn't say no."

We walked together out of the locker room, and then Ernie came out of the dugout and asked Stan and Tom to come down to the field. Stan stood with Tom while he was waiting to sing the national anthem.

Ernie started talking into the mic, "Welcome, everyone. We have a very special ceremony planned. I know it's not really baseball weather, but it's a sunny day here in Indianapolis, and I want to introduce to you nine very special Indianapolis alumni. Leading off, now living in West Bloomfield Township, Michigan, and playing right field, Roger Franciszek."

Ernie then introduced the other eight players.

"I also have two special young men here. If you get a chance, you may want to get their autographs because they're going to be future Detroit Tigers. First, the son of our right fielder, Stan "The Man" Franciszek."

The crowd clapped.

"Next, I have a young man who'll be singing the national anthem today, another future Detroit Tiger, Tom "The Machine" Mochina."

Tom stepped up to the mic and sang the National Anthem with a lot of passion. When he finished, the crowd stood and cheered.

Then Ernie announced, "Roger, would you like to say a few words?"

I walked to the mic, cleared my throat and started speaking. "I'm proud to be an Indianapolis Indian and so proud to be back on this field," I said. "But I'm not here to talk about baseball or myself. Almost sixteen years ago when I was playing here, I met a very special lady named

Louise. Louise, would you please come down to the field?"

Louise covered her face, but the people around her in the stands, as well as the other former players, encouraged her. I waited until she got near me before I continued.

"I was an okay ballplayer, but I was better at picking up women. This is probably why my backup, Roger Maris, made it to the majors, and I didn't. But I met this special lady, and I didn't realize how special she was. We ended up getting married, but I wasn't the best husband to her. She deserved a better husband, but she got me, and she has stuck by me a lot of years when most women wouldn't have. I almost lost her last summer, and I've realized that if I want to keep her for the next fifty years, I'd better start over and be a better husband. I still wish I could start over and make the major leagues, but I can't do that."

I got down on one knee. "Weezy, I can't make up for the past, but if you'll still have me, I want you to be my wife for the rest of our lives. I can't say I'll be perfect, but I pledge my love and support. You'll always be my queen, the lady I adore."

I pulled a ring box out of my pocket, which had a much bigger diamond than her current engagement ring. She put her hands over her heart as tears came down her cheeks. She started jumping up and down.

"Louise, you have your choice but I am asking you to be my wife all over again. I'll be a better husband than the deadbeat guy you've known."

She screamed yes, and we hugged. Everyone stood, clapped and cheered.

We took a bunch of pictures with Ernie Harwell. And because it was a couples occasion, I took a picture with Ernie and Louise. Stan took a picture with Shelley and Ernie. Tom took a picture with Teresa and Ernie. Eve took a picture with Bernie and Ernie. Then Louise's parents, who had come to watch, got their picture with Ernie, even though they'd probably never heard of him. As we turned to go, we could hear Ernie using his announcing voice.

"Wait a minute. Where are you going?" he asked. "There's a young lady with you who hasn't had a picture with me. Miss, would you please come here. What's your name?"

"Nancy," said Teresa's mom.

Ernie looked around and yelled, "Walt, I need you to come over here!"

A man about Teresa's mom's age walked over.

"Walt, this is Nancy. Isn't she beautiful?"

Walt looked at Nancy and said, "Quite beautiful."

"Everyone, this is Walt. He works in promotions with the Detroit Tigers, and he's single. Let's take a picture."

Teresa's mom, Ernie and Walt took a picture. After the picture, Walt and Teresa's mom kept talking.

Ernie, his wife and Walt had dinner with all of us at St. Elmo's Steakhouse, the place Louise and I had dinner after I found out she was pregnant. We all sat as couples—even Walt and Nancy—and we all ordered steak. It was really a treat for the kids who had very little experience with steak dinners. It was a great dinner and very special to have the voice of the Detroit Tigers with us.

When we got back to the hotel we all broke off as couples in the lobby, and I finally got a chance to talk to Louise alone.

"Roger, I can't believe you went to this much trouble to organize this. That was superb."

"Louise, I wanted to do something. I almost lost you. I wanted to do something really special to show you I wasn't trying to stay married for Stan, for the house or for financial reasons. I had to do something to show you it was you. I want to stay together always."

"How'd you get the participation from the others?"

"I reached out and told my story. We live in a world of too much divorce. I think they wanted to help me." I smiled. "Every ballplayer wants one more chance to get their name announced as a starter too."

"I love you, Roger."

"I love you, Louise."

> *"Us, us, us, us and them, them, them,*
> *And after all we're only ordinary men.*
> *Me, me, me, me and you, you, you,*
> *God knows it's not what we would choose to do."*
> — *Pink Floyd (1973)*

My Promise

"**M**om, when are we moving?"

"I don't know. I haven't talked to Bernie about that yet."

"Will I be able to work this summer? Can I stay with Gramps?"

"I'd like you to stay with me, Bernie and his children so we can start becoming a family."

"I really want to work this summer at Gramps' Docks with Teresa." I thought for a minute. "What school would I go to if we move to Dearborn?"

"Bernie said the public school is Dearborn Edsel Ford or you could go to Dearborn Divine Child, the Catholic school."

"Both seem like bad options to me. Five years ago, I had very few friends. Now I have a lot of friends. I've even become somewhat friends with The Joker.

"The Joker?"

"I now call Paul Barnes, The Joker." I smiled. "I really want to work with Gramps in the summers and go to Walled Lake Central."

"I know, Tom. It's all about what you want. You don't care about me. You don't appreciate that I'm trying to give you a family too. What am I going to do when you go off to college in three years?"

I just looked at her and could tell she was irritated with me. Maybe I was being selfish. Maybe I had to make this sacrifice. It just seemed so devastating to me.

For the remaining games of the basketball season, we would play every league team again and then play a game against West Bloomfield and our rivalry game with Walled Lake Western. We considered our record to be 6-5, and 4-0 in league play. However, I'm not sure if we were officially given credit for the Waterford win.

We started things off with the Farmington game. It was a close one, and we were down 44-43 with 20 seconds left in the game. Barnes scored on a layup coming off a Mark screen with seconds left, and we won the game. Barnes actually led the way with 15 points, and Mark and Kenny added 10 points each. Although it's been a tough season with Barnes, it was good to see him having a good game with his scoring and passing. It was also good to see Mark get his first double-digit-scoring game, comprised mainly of layups and put backs.

Next we had to play Waterford, and this time they had to come to our building. Coach Reese told us to just play basketball. The varsity and junior varsity coaches were going stand guard so there wouldn't be anything like what happened the last time.

Because Waterford didn't start anyone over six feet tall, the game plan was to go in to me on the block. If I got double teamed with either Mark's or Steve's man, I should look for them.

We dominated the game early and quickly figured out their strategy to foul me down low. Of the first five times I got the ball, I was able to score on three of those possessions even after getting fouled. I didn't set the world on fire with my free-throw shooting, but I did hit four of seven for a quick 10 points. After that I started looking to get Steve and Mark easy layups. When I got double teamed, I would pass to one of those guys cutting to the basket.

I kept my own statistics in my head, and I knew I had 12 points, 6 rebounds and 6 assists at halftime. We led the game 36-20, so I decided I was going to keep passing out of the low post and see if I could get the triple double.

By the end of the third quarter, I had 16 points, 9 rebounds and 10 assists. We were still up big, and Coach decided to sit me out.

With four minutes left to play, Coach Reese called me over and asked, "Would you like to jam one in a game?"

I knew he was talking about the illegal slam dunk. I just smiled. He put me back in the game.

On our first possession, Kenny took a jump shot. I moved around my defender and saw it hit the rim. I jumped up and grabbed it for the rebound with two hands and, in the same motion, I slammed it through. What a great feeling! The people watching the game came to their feet.

The referee immediately said no basket and gave me a technical foul. But it was worth it. I got a triple double by getting the rebound and a slam dunk all in one motion. Of course, I was the only one who knew about the triple double because I doubt there was anyone else counting assists.

Coach signaled for me to come back to the bench and put Jalkanen in the game. As I was coming to the bench, I heard a low voice come from the bleachers, "The Machine! The Machine! Way to ram it home! Yeah!"

I looked up and saw Denny yelling, and Floyd was right there next to him. I looked over a little farther and saw Teresa sitting with the girlfriends. She was smiling and clapping. None of them knew I might be moving soon. They were just enjoying the moment. I tried to do the same.

On Saturday I asked my mom if we could go to the Pontiac Mall. She agreed, and I went to the jewelry department at Montgomery Wards to buy a promise ring. I'd heard about promise rings on TV but didn't realize there were many different types. I bought one with a big purple oval stone. This would be my Valentine's Day present for Teresa.

On Tuesday, February thirteenth, I went to her house with my guitar after school, but before we started playing, I gave her the ring.

"T, this is a promise ring. My mother's getting married to Bernie, and it looks like I may have to move to Dearborn. I may not be able to work this summer, and I may have to go to school in Dearborn. But I promise you'll be my special girlfriend."

I could see she was pleased with the ring but very upset that I might have to move.

"I don't want you to move. Why didn't you tell me?" she cried.

"I'm sorry. I think I was in denial. I just can't believe it. I like Bernie, but I want to stay here.

As Teresa started to cry I said, "I'm sorry I had to tell you so close to Valentine's Day."

"I love the ring and will wear it proudly. You're the best boyfriend. Is there any way you can stay with someone in this area?"

"I asked that, and I was told I was being selfish. That's not what my mom wants. I've still got about four months, though, so let's enjoy our time together."

Teresa didn't really feel like playing guitars so we just sat together, talking and hugging. Teresa was so special. I'm not quite sure why she liked me but I was happy that she did.

The next two basketball games didn't go well for us. We got beat by Livonia Stevenson *and* Pontiac Northern. We played well against both teams but just got outscored. And losing these games cost us the conference title, which went to Pontiac Northern.

The next game against West Bloomfield was worst of all. They had three guys starting who were at least as tall as me. They blocked several of my shots, and I never really got rolling. We ended up getting beat by 39 points.

After we finished lunch, Stan looked over at me. I could tell something was on his mind.

"Tom, I really need to talk to you. Can we go for a walk?"

I agreed and we walked away from everyone else and down the corridor toward the gym.

"I won't be at basketball practice today, and I won't be at the game tomorrow against Western," Stan said.

"Hey, man, what is it?"

"The head baseball coach asked me to play shortstop on the varsity team this year, and he wants me to practice with the team today and play in the game tomorrow."

"What? That's great! I can't believe you didn't say anything at lunch."

"You and I have been on every team together since the baseball team four years ago. You're a great hitter—you're just as good a hitter as I am. But the coach wants me because I can play short. I was afraid to tell you 'cause you might not think this is fair."

"Stan, you've always been The Man. You've always been the best baseball player. I always wanted to hit like you. I'm glad you told me first, because I know I'll have to fight for the first base position on the freshman team. I'm going to work hard and try to join you in a couple years. I really wish I could come watch you play. As soon as our game gets done, I'll be out there. I'm proud of you. Thanks for telling me first, but let's go tell the guys."

"I want you guys to pound Western."

I smiled. "We will."

We walked back down and told everyone we could. I did most of the telling because Stan was a little shy in blowing his own horn. But I didn't mind. I really was proud of him. I'm not sure I'm ever going to be a professional baseball player, but I'll be the first one cheering for Stan when he makes the big leagues.

My report card came in the mail for my first semester in high school. I opened it to find I got an A in English I, Algebra I, Science I, French, Gym and Choir. I got a B+ in World Civilization, which resulted in a GPA of 3.9. I probably wasn't going to be the valedictorian because it was hard to compete with the others who didn't have quite so many extracurricular activities, but a top-ten finish wasn't out of reach. Even though I loved playing sports, I started to realize that going directly to professional baseball or getting a full-ride sports scholarship was not likely to occur. I was probably going to get to college on academics, so I needed to stay focused in class.

The next day, as we started warming up for the game against Walled Lake Western, I thought about Stan. He really wasn't getting a lot of playing time on the basketball team. I hoped he would play next year, but he would probably need the winter to get ready for baseball if he wasn't starting on the basketball team. He'd probably played his last high school basketball game. At least he'd be able to talk about his no-look pass to me to end the Pontiac Northern game.

Our starting lineup had become familiar, with Barnes and Kenny at guards, Mark and Steve at forwards and me at the post. We started this game with some unsuccessful pick and rolls, while Western had a shorter kid who was hitting shots from all over. Luckily, there was no three-point line back then, and these shots still only counted as two. Coach began subbing when we were down by 7 points in the first quarter.

I got back in the game with Kenny and Whitman at guards to start the second quarter. They both hit me with some good passes on the block, and I scored ten points. We trailed 32-30 at halftime.

In the second half, we kept feeding the ball down low, and I either took the post shot or hit Mark cutting for the basket. The problem was the kid on the Western team who kept hitting shots. We finished the third quarter tied at 48.

Coach Reese really wanted to win this game, so instead of making a lot of substitutions, he went with the starting lineup again. But Mark and Barnes had four fouls each, Steve had three and Kenny and I each had two. We played well and got the lead, but Mark picked up his fifth foul two minutes into the quarter, and then Barnes fouled out midway through. Larry played for Mark after that, and Stan would have been the logical choice for Barnes to possibly try to shut down their top shooter, but he was out playing baseball.

Coach decided to go with Whitman, the tennis player, instead, who had started the year as the last man on the bench. But he'd worked hard and become a good passer and tough defender. Whitman really hounded the Western sharp shooter. He also did a good job getting me the ball in the post, and we went up by eight points with a minute to go. Western started fouling us to try to extend the game, but we ended up winning 63-54. I finished with 19 points.

I congratulated all of the guys, and especially Whitman for the job he did. Then, instead of going to the locker room, Kenny and I hustled outside to try to catch Stan playing baseball.

We got there in the top of the sixth inning, and Stan was playing shortstop. Nothing got hit to him that inning, but he did throw the ball around the infield. Stan looked like he fit in even, though he was a little shorter than most of the guys.

We went over to the lady with the scorebook and saw that our team was up 4-1, but Stan was batting ninth and had struck out and grounded out in his two plate appearances. He was due to bat third in the bottom of the sixth inning.

The first player up from our team got hit in the back with the first pitch. That ball came in really fast. He didn't act like he was hurt, but I knew that had to sting. Maybe I wasn't ready for this league. He stared the pitcher down as he took first, and the second batter bunted for a sacrifice, moving the runner to second.

Stan came up next and hit from the left side as he's always done. He worked the count to 3-1. Stan was such a patient hitter. I would've been trying to hit by now. On the next pitch, he dragged a bunt down the first base line and got to the base before the first baseman could tag him. The runner made it to third.

"Good rap, number five!" I yelled.

"Number five's the man!" yelled Kenny.

Next the leadoff hitter was up. On the first pitch, Stan took off for second. The catcher bluffed but didn't throw to second to keep the other runner at third. The hitter worked the count to 2-2 and then hit a ground ball up the middle. Stan hustled in from second to score. He really looked good running the bases.

The game ended with our varsity team winning 6-1. Stan had gotten a hit, stolen a base and scored a run. A day before his fifteenth birthday, he was fitting in with some eighteen year-olds. I was impressed.

My birthday was only two days after Stan's. Even though I was a lot taller, he was chronologically older. For my birthday, my mother took Teresa, her mother and me to Big Boy. I got the Brawny Lad, fries and a root beer. Plus I had the brownie sundae for dessert. Afterward, we went back to Teresa's, and my mom talked a lot to Teresa's mom.

I knew the decision about our move was really bothering my mom. I knew she really loved Bernie—and me—so it was tough on her.

Teresa gave me a present in a small box.

"Tom, you gave me the promise ring, and I've decided I want to continue to be your girlfriend no matter where you move," she told me. "Promise rings are kind of girly, but I want you to have this as my promise to you."

I opened the box and saw a black ring that looked like it was hammered by a blacksmith. It was rough looking, just like I liked. On the inside, it read, *Yours, Teresa.*

"But there never seems to be enough time,
To do the things you want to do once you find them.
I've looked around enough to know,
That you're the one I want to go through time with."
— Jim Croce (1972)

Valentine's Day Eve

On Tuesday, I called Guy.

"Hello."

"Guy?"

"Hey, baby. We're still on for our Valentine's dinner tomorrow, right?"

I didn't respond to his question. "I want to talk to you," I said.

"Sure, what is it?"

"I just wanted to let you know that my surgery has all healed up."

"That's great. Is there anything else?"

"Yes, I'm not able to have any more children."

"I know, sweetheart. It's fine. Everything's good." There was silence and then Guy said, "So I'm picking you up at six tomorrow, right?"

I hesitated and then asked, "Why do you want to get married this spring when you know I can't have children?"

"'Cause I love you and want to spend every day with you. I want to raise the three kids we have together. Do you not love me?"

"I love you, but I was thinking I want to get married in 1976. It's good for people to date about four years before getting married."

"What? Why would you say that? I thought you wanted to be together?"

"I do ... in time."

"What's going on? Did I do something? Are you unsure of me? We've been planning this for over a month."

"I can't have children. How can I be a wife to you?"

"Eve, the day I proposed to you I knew you couldn't have children. What's the difference if we get married this year or in three years?"

I didn't know what to say. I just couldn't come out with it. But it seems I didn't have to.

"Wait a minute...Ah...You want to wait until Tom graduates so he doesn't have to change schools."

"Tom has a lot of friends."

"If that's it, why wouldn't you just tell me? Come on, we're engaged. We can tell each other anything. I want to get married, but I have a great job at Ford Motor Company. I can't move. "

"I know. Would it be okay if we didn't go out tomorrow night? I know I've disappointed you."

"You don't want to go out on Valentine's Day? So you want to stay engaged and wait three years?"

"Yes, I want what we have now."

"I want time to think about it. I guess it won't be such a happy Valentine's Day. Please give me time," he said sadly.

"Guy, I understand," I told him. "And I understand if you don't want to date for three more years."

—◆—

The next day I did receive a bouquet of roses at work with a card that read *I love you always, Guy*. I figured he'd ordered them before our conversation. Everyone who came by commented about the roses. However, I didn't hear from Guy on the day Americans celebrate love.

I felt heartbroken, but I'd been a mother for fifteen years, and I had to put my son first. I'd known Guy less than a year. How could I be 100% sure I could trust that he would love me when problems arose? How would he handle Tom really not liking Dearborn and missing his friends, his job and his teammates?

I didn't hear from him that next weekend either. I spent most of my time watching television. The only time I felt an uplift was when Sonny Elliott, the local weatherman, smiled and told me it was going to be a "clilly" day, his word to combine cloudy and chilly.

I wondered how Guy felt. Here I was feeling sad for myself, but I was the one who'd called off the wedding. I was the one who canceled our date for Valentine's Day. I was the one who told him I wouldn't move to his house. Was he at all sad or was he out trying to find another girlfriend?

On Wednesday, after I hadn't heard from him for a week, I decided to call him.

"Guy?"

"Hello, Eve," he said in a very monotone voice.

"Tom finished up basketball and started baseball."

"How'd he do against Western?"

"He had nineteen points and they won."

"Oh, that's great. I'm proud of him."

"Did you still want to date?"

"Of course, Eve. I love you. I just thought everything was going to work out, but I can see now that it would've been too tough on Tom. I was just all excited about being married, and I've had to work through the fact that it's not going to work out."

"I know. It's been tough on me too."

"When's Tom's next baseball game?"

"He has a home game next Tuesday after school."

"I'll try to make that."

Guy did come out to Tom's game. The coach didn't start him, and I could tell Tom wasn't happy. He sat on the end of the bench and didn't say a whole lot. This wasn't the Tom we were all used to. It had been a long time since he hadn't started a baseball game. He knew Guy was there, but Tom didn't really acknowledge either one of us.

Guy looked great. He really was the guy of my dreams. I wanted to smile and laugh with him, but I could tell Tom didn't really want us laughing. I wished there was some way we could've been married. There was no one else I wanted.

The coach put Tom in at first base for the last inning with the team up 5-2. He went out and played, but he still didn't seem very happy.

After the game we asked Tom if he wanted to go to Big Boy, and for the first time ever, he said he just wanted to go home. So Guy took us home, and then he went back to Dearborn.

The next week weekend Nancy, Teresa's mom, had asked Guy, Tom and me to meet her, Walt and Teresa at the Little Caesar's Sing-a-Long. They gave us song books, and we all sang together to some classic songs. Guy and Walt really seemed to like each other.

We started out with some fun-loving songs like "Down by the Riverside," but then they played "Won't You Come Home Bill Bailey," and I started to tear up thinking about Guy. Then they played "My Bonnie Lies Over the Ocean," and Guy turned to look at me. When they played "Have You Ever Been Lonely?" tears rolled down my cheeks.

"What is it, Eve?" asked Nancy.

I couldn't talk. I raised my right hand with my palm facing her and pointed to the inside of my hand. Then I pointed to an area about an inch lower. This was the Michigan way of indicating where I lived and where Guy lived. The inch represented many miles.

We excused ourselves to go to the ladies room, and I told Nancy we weren't getting married. She told me it was a good sign that he was still meeting up with me. She told me everything would be okay, but I didn't feel it. After I composed myself, we came back and ate pizza, but I didn't sing much.

After that I saw Guy about once a week. I enjoyed seeing him, but it was still a disappointment for both of us because we couldn't get married.

"Here I am on the road again.
Here I am up on the stage.
Here I go, playing star again.
There I go, turn the page."
— Bob Seger (1973)

Remembering Gramps

I heard my mother answer the phone and say, "Oh, no. Gramps? Is his wife there?"
Then after a moment she said, "Okay, Guy. I'll pray for him."

"Mom, who was that?" I asked.

"That was Bernie. He just took Gramps to the hospital."

"What?"

"He's getting old. He had a heart attack. They're trying to save him."

I was in disbelief. How could this be? I'd had no warning at all that Gramps might die. I thought a lot about him and decided I was going to give a talk at his funeral. I sat and wrote:

I don't know this guy you call Dr. Davis or Raymond or Ray, but I'm here today to talk about my very special friend, Gramps.

When I met Gramps five years ago, I had very few friends. I had failed at sports. I was angry. I was defensive. I was ready to fight anyone who did something I didn't like. Gramps was a busy professional who lived in a beautiful lake house with all the amenities. He had his own children and grandchildren. He didn't need to take time with some young boy who lived with only his mother in a tiny house, but he did.

He took a lot of time with me. He allowed me swim at his beach. He let me take his boats out. He let me sit on his picnic table. He talked to me. He started out telling me jokes, and bonding with me. He found a way to get me to listen to him. When I did listen, he taught me about relationships, communication and controlling my anxiety and anger. With his help, I became good at these life skills.

Thanks to Gramps, I now control my emotions, communicate well, have done well in three sports—four if you count horseshoes—have held a job, have been blessed with a lot of close friends and have a very special girlfriend.

Gramps, I miss you so much. I will always love you. Thank you for everything. My wish was that you'd see me become a successful adult, but now I know that whatever I do, wherever I go, I know you will be with me.

Your friend, Tommy Boy.

I didn't do anything else that night. I just thought about Gramps. A few hours later the phone rang again. My mother answered, and it was Bernie again. Was he calling to tell us Gramps had died? She hung up.

"How's Gramps?"

My mom smiled. "He's fine," she said. "He's coming home. It turns out his heart is in great condition."

"I thought he had a heart attack."

"Apparently so did Gramps, but when they checked him out at the hospital, all he had was gas."

"Gas?"

"He had such a severe gas reaction to something he ate that he thought he'd had a heart attack. But he didn't, and he's coming home."

I just couldn't believe it. It was too good to be true. Gramps was going to be fine. What an emotional roller coaster!

Baseball wasn't going as well as I'd have liked. I was hoping the coach already knew what kind of hitter I was, but while I was finishing up the basketball season, many other players were out competing for my spot at first base. It wasn't like I was playing for Stan's dad anymore. I had to prove myself.

I hadn't even started the first game, but in the second game, the coach batted me eighth in the lineup. I wasn't thrilled about this, but it was a lot better than not playing at all. My first time up I hit a line shot over the third baseman's head for a double. My second time up the pitcher threw me several curve balls and finally I got one that I could hit up the middle for base hit. In my third at-bat I got a fastball and hit it deep out to centerfield. Since there were no fences, I took off running. I raced for second and when I rounded the bag heading for third, and I saw everyone running in. As I got to third, the coach told me the centerfielder had caught the ball.

I was still two for three and thought I had showed the coach something, but I ended up sharing time with another first baseman for the season. I finally decided to just be happy about it and enjoy the season. I wasn't playing with Stan but Denny was the catcher about every other game, so it was fun playing with him. Kenny was on the team too, and he played leftfield almost every game.

We all had fun watching our friend play shortstop on the varsity team. Stan continued to bat ninth, but he got on base a lot and stole bases when he did. Every time there was a home varsity game, there were more freshmen there to cheer for Stan than the other fans combined.

On Saturday, March 10, Kay had a birthday party at her house in Golf Manner and invited her friends and all of us guys. This was the first time I'd been invited to a co-ed birthday party.

The snow had finally melted, so part of the party was outside. They didn't have horseshoes but they did have Jarts. Jarts was a game with projectiles that looked like huge darts. The object was to throw them into plastic circles about 18 inches in diameter. I got some of the guys to come out and play with me, and it turned out this game was fun, and I was good at it. Somehow my skills from horseshoes transferred. They ended up outlawing the game about fifteen years later for safety reasons, but we sure enjoyed it that day.

When we went back inside, the girls were playing Twister. It was fun just watching them fall all over each other, and I finally got to see Teresa and Kate in competition.

We had cake and ice cream while Kay opened her presents. She had asked us to each get her three of our favorite 45RPM records so she could have a big collection. I got her "Signs" by

The Five Man Electrical Band, "Doctor My Eyes" by Jackson Browne and "Turn the Page" by Bob Seger. It was fun to see what everyone else had picked out.

Next on the party agenda was playing Truth or Dare. Kay picked up the Twister mat and placed the spinner in the middle of the room. I was glad this wasn't going to be Spin the Bottle because we'd all have been in trouble. Kay spun to see who would go first, and it pointed toward Denny.

"Denny, you get to pick anyone," she told him.

"Okay, I pick Kay."

"You can ask anyone. You don't have to ask me."

"All right, fine. Kenny, who's the best athlete in our class?"

"Well this is a tough one, but I know the answer." He looked at me and then looked at Stan. "Sorry, guys, it's me!"

We all laughed, but he may have been right.

"Kenny, your turn."

"Kate, truth or dare. Who's a better kisser, me or The Machine?"

"Maybe I should take the dare." She laughed. "I've never kissed Tom. So, it's got to be you. Shelley, truth or dare. What is it about Stan that makes you come all the way out here?"

Shelley smiled and said, "Well, sorry girls, but I got to see Stan last summer without a shirt on. You can all eat your heart out. Floyd, who's the hottest girl in the class?"

"I better take the dare."

"What?" said Melanie.

"We have to make the game fun and take the dare once in a while," he said.

"Fine," said Shelley. "You won't tell Melanie she's the best looking girl, so sing 'You've Lost That Lovin' Feelin'" to her."

"I don't know it."

"You do so."

Floyd began in his deep bass voice, "You never close your eyes any more when I kiss your lips. And there's no tenderness any more in your fingertips..."

Everyone burst out laughing.

"Tom, truth or dare?

"What's your biggest fear?" Floyd asked.

"My biggest fear? You mean besides someone coming off the bench and grabbing my neck? My biggest fear?" I turned a little more serious. "My biggest fear is that my mom will get married and want me to move away from here."

"That would never happen. You can't move from here. I need the competition," said Kenny.

"Walled Lake Central would never be the same," said Denny.

"Hey, man, I'm hip. My biggest fear is that The Machine moves away too," said Floyd.

"Tom, you're up," said Kay.

"Melanie, truth or dare. What'd you think about Teresa when you first met her?"

"I better take the dare," she said, raising her eyebrows. "I'm taking the dare, but my first thought was 'here's some new girl Tom Mochina will probably start dating' and sure 'nough..."

"Hmmm. Act like a chimpanzee for two minutes," I said, laughing.

Melanie started bouncing around the room making chimp sounds and itching her sides. She was great, and it distracted everyone from my last truth.

"Your turn, Melanie," said Kay.

"Looks like it's time to ask Teresa. Teresa, truth or dare? If you won a million dollars, what would you do with it?"

"After that performance, I'll take the truth," she said with a smile. "I'd buy a Ford Mustang, ten new pairs of shoes, an electric guitar and a house for my mother in this school district. I'd still have a lot of money left, so I'd buy a house for Shelley and her mom out here too. Do I still have money? I'd buy Tom some decent shirts and find him a good hair stylist."

Everyone laughed.

"And if I still had money, I'd buy a lake house for Tom and his mom and convince that boyfriend of hers to move here."

—◆—

On Friday, March 16, Bernie came to our house and took a ride with my mother. They weren't gone long before they came back and asked if I wanted to go for a ride.

"Where are we going?"

"We want to show you something, and then Bernie said he'd get us a pizza."

"All right. Fine. I'll go anywhere for 'za."

I got in Bernie's truck, and we drove out to West Acres, the subdivision where Kenny lived. All of the houses were new. This was definitely one of the richer areas of the Walled Lake school system. It was close to Union Lake Elementary, Clifford H. Smart Junior High and closer than we were to Walled Lake Central.

Bernie stopped the car at a vacant lot that backed up to Middle Straights Lake. We got out and looked around.

"This is Middle Straights," I said. "I rowed over here once last summer. To get from Upper Straights to Middle Straights, you have to row under Green Lake Road. Why are we here?"

"I wanted to see if you liked this area."

"This is a great area. Kenny lives around here.

"Bernie bought this lot," said my mom.

"What? Why'd you buy this lot?"

"Ford approved my transfer to the Wixom plant, and I've always wanted to live out on the lake. I won't have to pay Gramps anymore for dock space."

"Bernie, I'll really miss you out at the docks, but you can take your boat under the road and come see me. I wish I could come live here with you," I said.

I looked at Bernie and my mom. They just smiled. "We're all going to live here? Wow, this would be a dream come true! This'll be great! Will we have a shower?"

Bernie kept smiling. "We have to approve plans for the house, but we're planning on having two showers. One for your mom and me, and one for you, Carl and Karen. We're planning on four bedrooms, so you can have your own."

"Oh, man, this is too cool. When will the house be built?"

"We don't know yet, but sometime in the summer. If we move in while you're still working, you can take the boat to work."

"The speed boat? Wow! But wait...I thought you two cancelled the wedding."

"We did. We knew you didn't want to move to Dearborn. But I want to be with you and your mom, so I put in for a transfer," Bernie explained. "This is a dream come true for me too. I'm going to leave it to your mother to see if we can still get the church for Memorial Day weekend. I know we can still have the reception at Gramps' Docks. I checked with him."

This was truly the best of all possibilities. I was in the school district. I'd have a shower. I'd live on the lake. My mom would be happy.

I haven't always had the best luck, but my mother has done a lot for me. I decided I was going to do everything I could to help make this new family work. I'd broken my mom and Bernie up once, but I wouldn't do it again.

"I'm really sorry for any trouble I caused the two of you," I told them. "Thank you. This means so much. We're going to be a great family."

The next weekend was Lucy's wedding. She was a beautiful bride, and Mark and Lucy both looked so happy. They had their reception at the VFW hall, and the dinner and wedding cake were delicious.

At one point in the evening, the announcer said, "For this next dance, I only want couples who are really happy."

Of course Lucy and Mark were out there, and Gramps and Mrs. Davis joined them. Gramps' daughter Mollie and her husband, as well as Gramps's son, Charlie, and his wife were out there too. My mom and Bernie followed, and Teresa's mom and Walt went out as well. Stan's mom and dad joined the dance, and then Stan and Shelley joined.

I looked around and saw all these happy couples. Then I looked at the girl I danced with. "Teresa, you're so beautiful. I'm so thankful to have you as my girlfriend and that we're among all these happy couples."

She smiled. "Don't tell the others, but we're the happiest of all."

After that I forgot there was anyone else in the world for the duration of the song."

Two significant events happened within a week of each other in 1973. On March 29, the last soldier left Vietnam, and on April 4, the World Trade Center in New York City opened. These two events gave me great hope that I would lead an adult life in peace, free of war. I thought we would never have another war. We were too smart for wars now. We'd be able to work everything out diplomatically, and the World Trade Center would help all nations work together.

At least those were my thoughts at the time. Things are never as simple as they might seem.

References &
Recommended Readings

Ellis, Albert. 1975. *A Guide to Rational Living*. Chatsworth, CA: Wilshire Book Company.

Ellis, Albert. 1997. *How to Control Your Anger Before It Controls You*. New York: Kensington Publishing Corp.

Gottman, John M. 1999. *The Seven Principles for Making Marriage Work*. New York: Three Rivers Press.

Gottman, John M, Gottman, Julie Schwartz & Declaire, Joan. 2006. *10 Lessons to Transform Your Marriage*. New York: Three Rivers Press.

Shaw, James. 2013. *The Baseball Bat: Learning to Control Anger and Anxiety with Help from Gramps*. Columbus, Ohio: A Slight Edge Publishing.

Shaw, James. 2014. *Defensive End: Learning More about Anxiety and Communication with Help from Gramps*. Columbus, Ohio: A Slight Edge Publishing.

Acknowledgments

John "JR" Ries – Thank you for your review suggestions and your insight into the flow of the story.

Jacqueline Nguyen – Your insight is priceless in pointing out many things from the female perspective. Your ideas get me thinking and helped tremendously.

Jessica Royer Ocken – You're an extraordinary editor.

Jim Render – Your art work is a great representation of what this book is about.

To everyone who has read this book – Thank you. It means a lot to me. I hope you also enjoyed *The Baseball Bat* and *Defensive End*.

To everyone who took the time to give me feedback or write a review publicly – Thank you. I value your feedback.

About the Author

James Shaw, PsyD, was born in Pontiac, Michigan, and lived in the metropolitan Detroit area through high school. He is now a licensed psychologist and clinical assistant professor at The Ohio State University Wexner Medical Center Family Practice.